INVISIBLE
WOMEN

INVISIBLE WOMEN

The Experiences of Undocumented Mexican Mothers Living in the U.S.

MARIA ALEX LOPEZ

SEPTEMBER, 2013

Library of Congress Control Number:		2013907828
ISBN:	Softcover	978-1-4633-5592-0
	Ebook	978-1-4633-5591-3

Rev. date: 24/09/2013

To order additional copies of this book, please contact:
Palibrio LLC
1663 Liberty Drive
Suite 200
Bloomington, IN 47403
Toll Free from the U.S.A 877.407.5847
Toll Free from Mexico 01.800.288.2243
Toll Free from Spain 900.866.949
From other International locations +1.812.671.9757
Fax: 01.812.355.1576
orders@palibrio.com
463565

CONTENTS

DEDICATION

I dedicate this book to my father, for his unconditional love, support, and faith in me. He encouraged me during my career and supported me in the hardest times.

ACKNOWLEDGEMENTS

I would like to thank Dr. Kathy Greenberg, for her constant support, guidance, and encouragement. She has been a great adviser and taught me a great deal on scientific research. I want to thank Dr. Sky Huck for his kindness. I, also, want to thank Dr. Howard Pollio for being an inspiration in my life. I admire his endless energy, brightness, and sense of humor. I would, also, like to extend my thanks to Dr. Velazquez for her passion working with Hispanic families. I was honored to work with these professors. Finally, I would like to thank the participants of this dissertation who made this possible. Thank you for allowing me to be part of your lives, sharing your experiences, your joys and hardships. Thank you for your trust, gratitude, and kindness.

ABSTRACT

This book is based on a phenomenological study on undocumented Mexican immigrant mothers of high school students who have lived in the U.S. for at least five years and received social services. Most of these mothers have emigrated from rural areas of the central and southern Mexican States of Guanajuato, Michoacan, Queretaro, among others. According to the participants, socio-economic conditions forced them to leave their homelands hoping to find a better life in the U.S.

Ten undocumented mothers of high school students living in the U.S. were interviewed from a phenomenological perspective. They were monolingual Spanish speakers (only one mother spoke a native Mexican dialect as a first language and Spanish as a second language), parents of several children, and unskilled laborers with little formal education. This book explored the experiences of these mothers, their beliefs and values, and their relationship with their children's school and the community in general. The outcomes confirmed some of the results presented in the literature review and revealed other findings that are critical to the development of school and social service programs.

CHAPTER ONE

INTRODUCTION

Give me your tired, your poor,
Your huddled masses yearning to breathe free,
The wretched refuse of your teeming shore.
Send these, the homeless, tempest-tossed to me,
I lift my lamp beside the golden door. Emma Lazarus

Undocumented: Seeking the American Dream

Each year thousands of undocumented immigrants try to cross the Mexican-U.S. border hoping for a better future for themselves and their families. Unfortunately, many of these immigrants die. Musician Ricardo Arjona from Guatemala wrote a beautiful song about undocumented immigrants called "El Mojado," the name that some people in the U.S. use to refer to undocumented immigrants crossing the Mexican-U.S. border. *Mojado* means "wet" in English and refers to the immigrants' backs being wet, from crossing the river (Rio Grande) when they arrive in the U.S. Arjona's song reflects the hardships immigrants face in their journeys. Hoping for a better life in the land of opportunity, some of these immigrants have found the so-called "American dream" has become the "American nightmare."

I can relate to this song for two main reasons: as an immigrant myself and as an advocate for undocumented people. The song is self-explanatory and uses direct language. Interestingly, the title of the song, "El Mojado" refers to a male immigrant. Traditionally, the man of the family comes to the U.S. by himself. After he settles down, gets a job, finds a place to live, and saves money for transportation, his wife and children join him.

Transportation includes hiring a "coyote," a person who crosses undocumented immigrants through the Mexico-U.S. border receiving a payment in exchange. However, research indicates, Mendoza (2002) that women are as likely as men to immigrate, and become part of the labor market.

The composer says, "His condition of transforming into the man he dreamed about and never achieved." Unable to meet their needs in their country of origin, undocumented people are excluded from a system that does not offer them chances. The author says "El mojado, the undocumented, carries the load that legal would never carry, not even forced." Undocumented people do the worst jobs in the U.S. They have to survive, they do not have options. They have to do whatever it takes to subsist, but if they were legal would never do these jobs. The song also reveals, "He is neither from here because his name does not appear in the files nor is he from over there because he left." Immigrating to a new country requires a huge adjustment that affects our identity. We are not from here, we are from another country, but we left our homelands so we no longer belong to that country. The sense of belonging that makes a person feel part of a group becomes questioned by the fact that we are not completely integrated into the new country and we are not physically present in our country of origin.

Very sadly, many times immigrants have to prove themselves. If I have to prove that I am trustworthy, honest, I cannot imagine how hard this experience is for people who do not have papers, education, or skills to access the labor market. I am from Buenos Aires, the capital and largest city of Argentina and the second-largest metropolitan area in South America, after Sao Pablo, Brazil. Based on the 2010 census, the city has more than two-million inhabitants while the province of Buenos Aires has more than fifteen millon inhabitants. However, I grew up in a relatively small neighborhood in which everybody knew me, my parents, and my grandparents; therefore, finding help when I needed it was relatively easy.

I came to the United States fourteen years ago. I underwent a huge adjustment period when I first arrived. Even though most people may think that the biggest barrier an immigrant must confront when moving to a new country is the language barrier, this is not always true, even when learning a new language is necessary. Instead, I believe the biggest obstacle is the culture tied to the language. When coming to the U.S., immigrants must prove they are good people who have come to this country to do good and to help others and that they are grateful for their achievements here. Unfortunately, undocumented people live in a survival mode and many times they do not have the chance to go to school, get a rewarding job, or achieve their goals.

As suggested in the song, lack of trust is a big factor: "Your truth tastes like lies; your anxiety tastes like sadness." It is human nature for people to trust what they know, rather than what they do not know. I can understand such skepticism, even with people from the same country. However, compounding this problem, the stereotype of Hispanic immigrants has played an unfavorable role in the acceptance of immigrants. Undocumented immigrants have been characterized in the media with some negative characteristics. For example, in the movie *Up in Smoke* (1978), the two characters, "Cheech" and "Chong," are undocumented Mexican immigrants. They are uneducated, lazy, drug users, who drive a van smuggling marijuana from Mexico to the U.S.

The negative perceptions of undocumented immigrants, and Mexican immigrants in particular, labeling them as *illegal immigrants*, equating their immigration status to crime, and prosecuting them, harmfully affected the immigration process of millions of people whose only purpose for being in this country is to work hard and prosper. This book, however, is based on the experiences of undocumented mothers. I was particularly intrigued about the lives of these women, who come to the U.S. either by themselves or with their husbands and children, trying to find a better life.

My Experience Working with Undocumented Families

I worked as a bilingual therapist at a contracted social service agency for three years. This agency provided counseling services to the Department of Children Services (DCS). Working as a social service therapist was a challenging experience that gave me the opportunity to learn more about immigration issues and helped me to understand some of the struggles undocumented immigrant mothers face in their journey. Though I had experience in the fields of psychology and education, working in social services with undocumented immigrants was a completely different experience.

As an immigrant and as a therapist, I am always interested in learning about and understanding immigrant groups and their needs, as well as finding efficient ways of assisting them to make a difference in their lives. Having worked with Hispanics here in the U.S., I found that, although often eager to receive help, they are very reluctant to seek services of any kind, whether legal, medical, or social. I feel they are distrustful of providers for many reasons, including being frightened because of their immigration status and because they do not have a command of the English language. Seeking services may be embarrassing and frustrating to them. Furthermore, they were unfamiliar with the social service organizations in the U.S.

Clients were referred to the social service agency from DCS. Because of legal reasons, some clients were court ordered to receive services and comply with the assigned treatment. For example, if a client was placed on probation, he/she had to meet several requirements to be released from probation, depending on the problem, such as anger management classes, alcohol and drug education classes, or family counseling. Clients with their children at risk of entering State custody, or already in State custody, had to complete either a safety or a permanency plan that included several requirements depending on their specific problems such as parenting skill classes, individual counseling, drug test screens, getting a job, or moving to a new house.

These legal or administrative issues interfered with the therapeutic process. In fact, working with these clients, I found that most of these clients, only complied with treatment to get what they wanted, either their children back home, or get rid of DCS, probation officers, and court citations. In other words, most of these clients did not see counseling as a helpful tool to improve their lives. This is not to say that the legal aspect is not important, only that its nature is not part of the counseling process, and therefore, the client questioned the legitimacy of the services. According to Sandler, Dreher, Dare, & Holder (1973), the therapist-client relationship plays an important role in the psychotherapy process. When a client demands treatment, he/she is asking for help in the person of the therapist. On the contrary, when the client is not asking for help and the therapist goes to the client's house, without any indication from the client that help is needed, resistance may take place. Fortunately, some clients agreed to receive help, beside the fact that there were obligated to receive services, but in my professional experience, some clients were skeptical, distrustful, and even combative in the presence of the therapist. It was a personal and private space after all that was invaded by someone without the client consent.

Resistance:

During the initial part of treatment, some clients became very resistant to receive services. Some of them created excuses to cancel appointments, tried to avoid me by not answering the phone, and lied to me to skip a random drug test. Most of them changed their attitudes in a relatively short period of time, two or three weeks, sometimes longer. Although I am Hispanic, they did not trust me immediately, but when they trusted me, they really trusted me. They called me on my work cell phone; felt more comfortable discussing their issues; and for a short time, shared with me some of the most meaningful aspects of their family life.

My main responsibility as a therapist was to assist at-risk families with children in crisis in an effort to preserve the family unit. Some of the most common issues presented during the sessions were truancy, domestic violence, and substance abuse, but some of these families needed services that exceeded the traditional role of a therapist. Most of these clients were unable to communicate in English, particularly with schools and in general, causing a strong sense of isolation and detachment from the mainstream community. Their unawareness of the school rules, their immigration status limiting their job opportunities, and their everyday battles raising their kids in a foreign country, make them a group with special needs that some social service agencies cannot meet.

Resistance affected the length of services and was expressed in different ways such as cancelling or rescheduling appointments, not returning phone calls, being oppositional or argumentative. However, resistance cannot be measured by the times clients were not available for their sessions. Some clients showed up but did not comply with the treatment. They could not make changes in their lives, including behaviors, relationships, education, finances, or lifestyle choices. Even though they were aware of their problems, they could not change anything in their lives. Some clients showed lack of motivation, fear to change, and lack of a supportive and positive network, which could have contributed to their resistance to change.

Most of these clients were referred for mental health and/or substance abuse problems. Padilla & Ruiz (1973), states that Hispanic women tend to be very private about mental health problems. They are very reluctant to discuss health problems with other people including doctors and therapists. Given that the majority of undocumented Hispanic immigrants in the U.S. are socio-economically disadvantaged, and face a language barrier that keeps them from the media about the prevalence of mental health and substance abuse, many do not realize that they have a problem and that help is available, nor do they know that some Spanish-speaking professionals, like myself, want to help them with an individualized, culturally specific treatment plan. A brief description of my job will provide a better understanding of some of the needs of undocumented immigrants.

Serving the Undocumented—Social Service Counseling:

Services were provided in the client's home. Once receiving a case, a social worker from DCS was contacted within 24 hours and the client within 48 hours. Usually, the first contact with the client was by phone to schedule an appointment at the client's home. However, some of our clients did not have a phone, so the therapist went to the client's house. As I mentioned before, delivering services at the client's house is difficult for therapists. Working with undocumented immigrants reinforced my awareness of this discomfort. Clients did not know the functions of U.S. organizations. They were concerned about confidentiality and their immigration status, and some agencies did not have Spanish-speaking therapists, therefore, the language barrier created more intimidation to the client. Undocumented immigrants did not know what DCS or any government agency did. The lack of Spanish-speaking therapists and interpreters impeded them to communicate with health workers. Compounding this problem, some English-speaking therapists refused to use interpreters with Spanish-speaking clients because it violates confidentiality.

Getting to Know the Clients:

The first meeting is one of the most important parts of the treatment. The main goal in the first meeting is getting to know the client and developing a good rapport. During the first meeting, therapists introduce themselves, explain the services provided, and complete several forms as part of documentation, which is an important part in delivering social services. To avoid potential liability risks, social service therapists must submit up-to-date documentation showing proof of the services provided. For those who are not completely familiar with documentation, it includes the client's rights, consent for treatment, psychosocial assessments, confidentiality form, and release and request forms.

Therapists gather relevant information through the documentation process that helps them understand the client and his/her needs. Gathering information from undocumented immigrants, however, is one of the most difficult areas of treatment. First, therapists had to read in English and translate to the clients at the same time. Documentation forms were not available in Spanish (only English). Second, because most of these clients have little or no formal education, they were unfamiliar with most of the words and could not understand some of the statements included in the documentation. Part of the therapist's job is to break each sentence down and reword it in simple terms to ensure that the client understands the paperwork's content.

Another important part of the documentation process is the treatment plan. The therapist, along with the client, developed the treatment goals with the current date and a target date for completion, usually within three months. If the client did not meet the goals included in their treatment plan during the three months, or needed additional help, a new treatment plan was developed. In addition, most of the documentation process occurs during the first session, when the relationship with the client has not been established. Therefore, the therapist must conduct the interview in a friendly but firm manner, offering a clear explanation about the services, and ensuring the client that the therapist's main goal is to assist them. Social service therapists, especially when working with undocumented immigrants, advocate for their clients, offering relevant information to make them feel as comfortable as possible.

Additional distress is created by the clients' initial inability to understand the nature of the therapist's job. Aware of this situation, I made a conscientious effort to provide information that included clear, simple, and unambiguous terms. I found that building a good relationship between the therapist and the client by showing honesty and consistency was important in the therapy process and makes the clients feel safer and more comfortable. The following section includes a real case to illustrate the role of resistance in the counseling process.

Working with Angry Clients:

This section includes a brief summary of a former client's case that illustrates the role that resistance plays in the therapeutic process.

Two sisters were accused of drug issues and environmental neglect. A family member filed a complaint against them. The report said the sisters were using and selling drugs, lived in a dirty and unhealthy house with 12 cats, and the children were playing with the cats' feces. They lived with three kids. I received the case, made an appointment over the phone, and went to the house. One of the sisters seemed very angry. She was extremely rude, neither saying hello nor wanting to talk to me. When I tried to talk with her, she asked me to leave the house. I could understand her anger. She did not want a social service therapist checking her house. However, we therapists were instructed to leave the client's houses when clients refused services. I was ready to leave their house but the other sister tried to smooth things out so I agreed to work with her.

The two sisters had to take two drug tests to prove they were not using drugs. These tests were conducted by randomly dropping by their houses, where they took the tests. When clients know they have a drug-test appointment, they do not take drugs during that week or month, depending on their drug of choice. Some drugs take longer to leave the system. After a couple of weeks, they took the tests and passed them. I was supposed to close the case at that time; however, I did not feel comfortable doing so. The house was dirty and untidy with clothes, pieces of food, toys, and garbage everywhere. The children were also extremely dirty. Although these clients were not using drugs, at least during the time they were tested, their children were living in a house that did not meet minimum standards.

The three months were over and I had to close the case,
unless something about drugs came up.

This case also illustrates limitations. Because these sisters were hostile and not willing to change their lifestyle, there was no sense in referring them to parenting classes or providing homemaking services. They were not interested in our services.

Cultural Awareness:

Some of the questions that motivated me to write this book were the following: *What is Cultural Awareness? Am I culturally aware that my clients have a particular and singular experience which is different from my own experience?*

Cultural awareness is one of the most important skills to have as a social service therapist, particularly when interacting with undocumented immigrants. Working with Mexican mothers made me more aware of this issue. Hispanics come from different places and have diverse backgrounds. Most of my clients were from Mexico, Guatemala, and other Latin America's countries. We are all called *Hispanics* or *Latinos* as a homogeneous group, perhaps because people assume that we all speak Spanish or that we all have dark hair, dark eyes, and brown skin, disregarding cultural differences in the Hispanic population that may include people from a Latin America's country like Mexico, a European country like Spain, or a Caribbean country like Cuba, or people who grew up in a big metropolitan city or a little rural town, or may include people who speak Spanish or native dialects like Tarasco. For example, a person from a rural area in Mexico, who speaks a native dialect, does not have much in common with a person from Madrid, Spain, which is a metropolitan, cosmopolitan city. People call them both Hispanics. Valdivieso & Siobhan (1992) state,

> *In fact, the term "Hispanic" was created by the Federal*
> *bureaucracy as a means of labeling a category that*
> *included several groups. "Latino" derives from Latin*
> *America, a term devised to distinguish Spanish and*

Portuguese colonized American lands from those American lands colonized by Northern Europeans. The first widespread use of "Latin", apart from the geographical designation, denoted certain kinds of music, as in the phrase "a Latin beat." Only recently, has Latino been proposed as an alternative to "Hispanic," largely by proponents of Hispanic unity movements (p.5).

Also, awareness of social class and lifestyle differences is important by understanding the cultural background, beliefs and values, preferences, and priorities of clients. The following case clarifies the role that cultural awareness plays in working with undocumented families.

Working with Victims of Sexual Abuse:

A 12-year-old girl was raped by her cousin and became pregnant. The family was devastated. It was very hard to talk with them. Her parents said they did not trust anybody. They did not speak English. The fact that I spoke Spanish made them feel somewhat better, but they were still uncomfortable. Every time the mother had an appointment, she asked me, "Are you going to ask me questions?" She was very defensive and skeptical. Completing documentation was very difficult. I had to break every question down and make them simpler. I explained to them the services to be provided. The family was undocumented and feared to be deported. I told them that I was there to help them in any way possible regardless of their immigration status.

As a therapist, I provided individual and family therapy sessions, along with parenting skill classes. I taught her how to bathe a baby using a doll, and changing diapers, when she was supposed to be at school. It was hard to explore some areas of their lives. They were completely hermetic. During a session, the mother said they thought about giving the baby up for adoption, suggesting somebody told them to do so. I explained to them that they were the only ones—(the 12-year-old and her family—to decide what to do with the baby. Nobody had the right to push them. After a couple of months working together, the baby was born two months prematurely, and they decided to keep her. During delivery, the 12-year-old mother was diagnosed with pneumonia. After she left the hospital, she was referred to different agencies in the community to ensure she was safe, and the case was closed.

This case illustrates how cultural differences affect interaction with clients. The mother was a submissive person. Every time I asked her a question, she looked at her husband, who responded to me. I respectfully gathered the needed information and did not question such interaction, seeing no point in attempting to remake a lifestyle in a period of six months. The family lived in a small apartment with several members of their extended family. Both parents worked full time. Tragically, one of the extended family members raped their 12-year-old daughter. When I advised the mother to ensure that her daughter was safe, she nodded her head, looked down, barely making eye contact with me.

The case illustrates the challenges that therapists face when working with immigrant clients. Understanding cultural differences helps therapists provide competent services. One of the main concerns I had as a therapist was: *How can I help this person or family?* The case, also, illustrates, from the client's perspective, the overwhelming adjustment that undocumented immigrants face when coming to the U.S.

Purpose of this book

The purpose of this book is to explore the lived experiences of undocumented immigrant mothers of high school students who lived in the U.S. and received social services. During my years working as a social-service therapist, I had several concerns. I wondered about the main obstacles that these mothers faced in the U.S. Besides their joys, hopes, and dreams, I wondered about the things they were missing that kept them from being successful in this country. Ten undocumented mothers, former clients of a social service agency, were selected to participate in this book. Most of these immigrants were monolingual Spanish speakers, parents of several children, and unskilled laborers with little education.

According to the participants, socioeconomic conditions forced them to leave their homelands—rural areas of the central and southern Mexican States of Guanajuato, Michoacan, and Queretaro, among others—hoping to find a better life in the U.S. The main question of this book which made me explore and research on these mothers is "What are the experiences of undocumented Mexican mothers of high school students living in the U.S. who received social services?" The literature contains revealing findings from many research studies—most of which are not qualitative and do not explore the lived experiences of undocumented immigrants—but are extremely helpful and an invaluable complement to qualitative research. I chose to use phenomenology as the theoretical framework, to give my participants a voice, the same voices that have been unheard for decades.

Methodology

Unlike other qualitative methods that focus on data contrast, existential phenomenology seeks to understand the essence of an experience through an exhaustive and deep analysis of the phenomenon. Phenomenology allows for questions related to the core of the experience. Valle & Halling (1989) state, "When applied more specifically to human psychological phenomena, existential phenomenology became *existential-phenomenological psychology,* and, as such has become that psychological discipline that seeks to explicate the *essence, structure,* or *form* or both human experience and human behavior as revealed through *essentially* descriptive techniques including disciplined reflection" (p.7).

Review of Literature regarding
Undocumented Mexican Immigrants

According to Passel & Cohn (2008), a large majority of immigrants arriving in the U.S. in the recent past are undocumented with 80% to 85% of Mexicans in the U.S. for less than a decade being undocumented. Among all foreign-born Mexicans in the country, more than half (56%) are estimated to be unauthorized. The terms *undocumented immigrants* and *unauthorized immigrants* are interchangeably used by different authors to refer to an immigrant from Mexico or elsewhere that does not have U.S. documents. However, most authors prefer the term *illegal immigrants* in referring to immigrants that came to the U.S. without proper papers.

Aware that language is the tool to communicate our ideas and beliefs, I choose to use the term *undocumented* instead of *illegal*. I think the term *illegal* has a criminal implication. I, also, think that undocumented people are not breaking the law in a criminal way. Undocumented immigrants do not have papers or documents to prove they are authorized to live and work in the U.S., but that situation does not make them criminals. Instead, I see it as an administrative issue or a consequence of their country economic problems.

Research indicates (Chang, 2008; Bacon, 2008) that the U.S. signed several international agreements with Mexico and other Latin America's countries, including NAFTA, the Bracero program, which allowed immigrants to enter the U.S, but after their work visas expired, these immigrants were sent back to their countries. Being excluded from a country that did not provide them the opportunity to meet their basic needs, they were forced to leave in order to survive, and then expelled from the new country.

Defining Undocumented Immigrants
Who are the Mojados?

The study of immigration is a complex phenomenon, including such factors as the immigrants' socioeconomic background, educational level, knowledge of the new country's language, and immigration status. According to the U.S. Department of Homeland Security, (Hoefer, Rytina, & Baker, 2009), the foreign-born population, defined as the people living in the United States who were not U.S. citizens at birth, consists of five categories:

(a) *Legal permanent residents* (LPRs), also known as *green card* recipients have been granted lawful permanent residence in the United States.

(b) *Refugees* and *asylees* are persons who sought residence in the United States to avoid persecution in their country of origin. Persons granted refugee status applied for admission while outside the United Sates. (In contrast, persons granted asylum applied at port of entry or after entering the United States).

(c) *Naturalized citizens* are foreign-born persons ages 18 and over who have become citizens of the United States. Most legal permanent residents are eligible to apply for naturalization after five years of obtaining LPR status.

(d) *Nonimmigrants* are authorized to stay in the United States for a limited time. Most nonimmigrants enter the United States as tourists or business travelers. Others come to work, study, or engage in cultural exchange programs.

(e) *Unauthorized resident immigrant population or undocumented immigrants* are defined as all foreign-born non-citizens who are not legal residents. Most unauthorized residents either entered the United States without inspection or were admitted temporarily and stayed past the date they were required to leave. Unauthorized immigrants applying for adjustment to lawful permanent resident status under the Immigration and Nationality Act (INA) Section 245(i) are unauthorized until they have been granted LPR status, even though they may have been authorized to work. Persons who are beneficiaries of Temporary Protected Status (TPS)—an estimated several hundred thousand—are not technically unauthorized but were excluded from the legally resident immigrant population because data are unavailable in sufficient detail to estimate this population.

Increasing Numbers

An increasing number of undocumented Mexican immigrants have been settling in the U.S. during the last ten years. According to the 2010 Census, 308.7 million people resided in the United States on April, 2010, of which 50.5 million (or 16 percent) were of Hispanic or Latino origin. The Hispanic population increased from 35.3 million in 2000 when this group made up 13 percent of the total population.

According to Camarota (2012),

> Immigration has clearly played an important role in American history. The immigrant population in 2010 was double that of 1990, nearly triple that of 1980, and quadruple that of 1970, when it stood at 9.6 million. The increase in the size of the immigrant population has been so dramatic (20.2 million) in the last two decades that just this growth is double the size of the entire foreign-born population in 1970 or even 1900 (page 9).

However, the number of undocumented immigrants still remains unclear. In fact, the U.S. government launched a national campaign encouraging undocumented immigrants participate in the 2010 census. According to the U.S. government, the Federal law protects these immigrants' confidentiality. The U.S. Department of Homeland Security, (Hoefer, Rytina, & Baker, 2009), states that the unauthorized resident population is the remainder or "residual" after estimates of the legally resident foreign-born population—legal permanent residents (LPRs), asylees, refugees and nonimmigrants—are subtracted from estimates of the total foreign-born population. Data to estimate the legally resident population were obtained primarily from the Department of Homeland Security (DHS) while the American Community Survey (ACS) of the U.S. Census Bureau was the source for estimates of the total foreign-born population.

<u>Mexicans are the largest group:</u>

Even though the 2010 census shows that today's immigration is more diverse than ever, diversity among the foreign born has declined significantly. One country—Mexico—and one region—Spanish-speaking Latin America—dominated U.S. immigration, including documented and undocumented, during the decade. According to the 2010 census, Mexico alone accounted for 54% of the growth in the foreign-born population and had the largest numeric change (11.2 million), growing from 20.6 million in 2000 to 31.8 million in 2010. Mexicans accounted for about three-quarters of the 15.2 million increased in the Hispanic population from 2000 to 2010. The decline of diversity occurred not only at the national level, but also in many states, most significantly in Arkansas, North Carolina, Georgia, Indiana, Tennessee, Utah, Nebraska, and Alabama.

The Economics of Undocumented Workers

A global economic crisis, especially in developing countries of Latin America like Mexico, forces their citizens to leave their homelands to survive. The movie *In the air and Sun* (En el aire y el sol), released in 2007 and directed by Anne Lewis, illustrates the corporate power and the socioeconomic circumstances workers face everyday in Morristown, a city with a 15.8% of Hispanics based on the 2010 census. In a brief synthesis, the documentary shows how several companies moved from the northern states of the U.S. to the southern states of the U.S., to avoid unions and union wages. Fortunately, workers remained united, became a stable working class, and won union contracts. In the 1970's, however, that changed, and corporations realized that sending their factories to Mexico was more profitable, closed several plants in Morristown, and thousands of workers became unemployed. Different corporations installed the *maquiladoras*, also known as *in-bond companies* or *twin plants,* which are a type of customs-privileged facility that originated in Mexico in the 1960s and provides U.S. companies with a favorable means to use low-cost Mexican labor. They operated through an agreement with the Mexican government allowing U.S. companies to import parts and materials into Mexico without import taxes provided the finished products are re-exported to the United States or another country.

This created numerous jobs for Mexicans, and even though the cost of living in Mexico was considerably lower than the cost of living in the U.S., skilled workers were paid $1 or $2 dollars an hour, which put them below the line of poverty. This situation forced Mexican workers to leave their country. However, once in the U.S., they found inequity, exploitation, and abuse. Undocumented workers have very limited options here in the U.S. They will take *back breaking jobs* in order to survive. Usually they accept low paid jobs in farms, factories, construction, or fast food restaurants. The movie shows undocumented Mexicans working under the most excruciating conditions on farms as tomato pickers. For the past 18-20 years, these workers have received the same level of low pay, about 40 cents per bucket. According to this documentary, some undocumented workers employed in factories worked between 10-12 hours a day, without taking any breaks, and they were exposed to denigrating conditions.

Studies on Undocumented Mexican Women

When reviewing the literature on undocumented Mexican immigrants, I found several qualitative studies on undocumented Mexican mothers living in the U.S., which included relevant information related to this population. The main aspects described in the literature were immigration status, cultural values, language barrier, accessing social services, and exclusion. One of the most challenging situations immigrants face when immigrating to the U.S. is the conflict between their cultural values and the new country values. Mendoza

(2002) states that Mexican immigrant women living in the U.S. find it difficult to adapt to the new culture. Rules and values are different in the U.S. and the adjustment period is often painful. The author stresses the value of the extended family in Latin America's countries like Mexico, which is composed of three generations and closely tied. According to Mendoza, women worry about losing the close connection they had with their family members and their children, who imitate their American friends maintaining "cold and distant" relationships, communicate in English, and are highly influenced by their peers.

In Barnes' qualitative research (1969), the author points the difficulties that Mexican women find when immigrating to the U.S., in the first few years after arriving. He states that in traditional Mexican culture, in all classes, the family *is the focus of social identification and a sanctuary in a hostile world*. When coming to the U.S., Mexican women experience a huge period of adjustment, their family life becomes different, and they find it very difficult to adjust to the new rules. Bressler (1996) studied the lives of immigrant women in Pennsylvania. She states that migrant women do housework and work in the farm labor camps as well. The author states that the traditional family structure changes in the U.S. In the Mexican family and other Hispanic families, the older children are to babysit their younger siblings. The availability of day care centers reduces the pressure to serve as surrogate mothers for the younger children in the household. According to this author, Hispanic children can decide either to continue or quit school. Bressler, also, describes Mexican women as strong and resilient, having the courage to move and support their families. Hancock (2007) describes the difficulty that undocumented (sin papeles) women from rural areas of Mexico face when coming to the U.S. The author states that these immigrant women come from poor families, are uneducated, and place family as the center of their lives. She, also, states that being a mother is regarded in the Mexican culture as an integral part of a woman's identity, therefore, women who adhere to an individualistic approach, gaining personal autonomy and independence when coming to the

U.S., are often disapproved of by their family members, specially their spouses who perceive this change as a loss of interpersonal power.

According to Machado-Casas (2002), the disconnection Mexican women experience from the mainstream community creates a strong sense of isolation. She describes in her article the lived experiences of undocumented indigenous immigrants from Mexico, El Salvador, and Guatemala, who speak a native dialect from their places of origin instead, and experience a great level of isolation. She states that the disconnection between the U.S. society and these immigrants' needs continues to keep them isolated from the community. The author stresses that these immigrants come from a historical tradition of passing on knowledge and survival wisdom.

Several research studies (Horton, 2008; Hondagneu-Sotelo, 1996) state that one of the most difficult situations that undocumented immigrants face is the separation from their children. When coming to the U.S., depending on the situation, several factors such as fear to cross the border or financial problems, force these mothers to leave their children in their home country. Horton (2008), in a study on transnational motherhood, states that undocumented immigrants who have left their children at home endure a shared citizenship, they work here in the U.S. but are mothers there in Mexico or their country of origin. Globalization separates reproduction from production. Being a transnational family has a tremendous effect on these families transforming the gender roles and the family dynamic.

Willen (2007) describes the lived experiences of undocumented immigrant mothers in the U.S. The author states that the study of "illegality" transcends the legal frame, and alerts us about the effects that "illegality" has on undocumented families and their being-in-the-world. Willen urges researchers to examine "illegality" not as a sociohistorical construct, but as an embodied experience. Villenas (2001) indicates that undocumented

Mexican women living in the U.S. are one of the most vulnerable immigrant groups. They struggle to be part of the new society, working to support their families, assisting their children in school, attending English as a Second Language (ESL) classes, but are seen by the community as "problems" or "victims". The author indicates,

> Their culture and language were a "problem" while their gender made them "victims" of the stereotyped Latino machismo. In the practice of benevolent racisms, they were also constructed as "needy"—needing English, parenting skills, and health care—and "lacking"—wanting language, cleanliness, adequate housing, and, most of all, knowledge of how to raise and educate their children in a "modern" way (p.8).

Belliveau (2007), states that undocumented mothers are excluded from the social benefits their U.S.-born children are eligible to receive. The author describes the experiences of undocumented mothers with policies that exclude them from any benefit. Participants of this study shared their experiences on accessing the labor market, social services, and education. They shared feelings of isolation and exclusion and stated that the root of their problems was their lack of documents. McClelland & Chen (1997), describe the experiences of undocumented mothers communicating with the school. These mothers were monolingual (Spanish) and communicated with the school staff who only spoke English. One participant was singled out to explore her experiences standing up for her son. The main findings of this study were: (a) "I do not understand what is going on at school," (b) "The school is difficult to deal with," and (c) "Others wonder what I am doing at school."

The literature included in this section offers valuable information about undocumented Mexican mothers. It is important to notice, however, that participants selected for this book were former clients of a social service agency. They were facing individual or family crisis and some families had children who were at risk of entering State custody. The understanding of the family dynamic is crucial in the therapy process. Families in crisis require a specific intervention, which is a short term, intensive, goal-focused therapy approach. During the first interviews, the therapist identifies the main problems the family is dealing with, and creates a treatment plan. This kind of intervention usually lasted between one to three months. Clients who needed more assistance or desired to continue treatment were referred to different places in the community to receive further psychotherapy services.

Bonnefil & Jacobson (1979), state that family crisis intervention is based on crisis theory and includes the use of individual crisis intervention. The usual emphasis with children and young adolescents in crisis is on helping their parents to help them. The goal of this intervention is to identify the main problems and find the inner and outer resources of the family and its members. Flannery & Everly (2000), indicate that even though there are different models of crisis intervention, there is an agreement on the general principles applied. They synthesize the main principles: (a) Intervene immediately, (b) Stabilize, (c) Facilitate understanding, (d) Focus on problem-solving, and (e) Encourage self reliance.

Significance of the Study

This book is significant to the domains of educational psychology and social work as it extends the fields' current knowledge base. The book addresses unanswered questions that will help educators, social workers, and therapists, among others, to understand undocumented immigrants' needs, desires, and expectations as a first step toward providing culturally competent social services.

Limitation of the Study

This book is a phenomenological exploration of the lives of ten undocumented mothers living in the U.S. The most important limitation to consider is the sample size. This specific type of research does not allow generalization to a larger population of undocumented Mexican mothers but it provides revealing information in the study of these participants.

Organization of this Book

This book includes five chapters: Chapter One includes the introduction, definition of undocumented immigrants, statement of the problem, the research method, purpose, significance, and limitations of the study. The chapter also includes the research question: "What are the experiences of Undocumented Mexican Mothers of High School Students Living in the U.S. and receiving social services?" Chapter Two includes a review of the literature about undocumented immigrants living in the U.S. by examining the following: Perceptions about undocumented immigrants, Mexican immigrant women, education of immigrant children, and parental involvement. Chapter Three discusses the presentation of the research question, site and participants, introduction of participants with their biographies, rationale for a phenomenological research, and research procedures. Chapter Four includes an analysis of the results along with the ground and emerging themes from the interview outcomes. Chapter Five includes conclusions, implications, recommendations, areas for future research, and personal reflections.

CHAPTER TWO

REVIEW OF LITERATURE

Utopia lies at the horizon.
When I draw nearer by two steps, it retreats two steps.
If I proceed ten steps forward, it swiftly slips ten steps ahead.
No matter how far I go, I can never reach it.
What, then, is the purpose of utopia?
It is to cause us to advance.
Eduardo Galeano

This chapter reviews the literature on undocumented immigrants living in the U.S. by examining the following topics: perceptions about undocumented immigrants, Mexican immigrant women, education of immigrant children, and parental involvement. This review is related to the research question, "What are the Experiences of Undocumented Mexican Mothers of high school students living in the U.S. who received social services?"

Perceptions about Undocumented Immigrants

During the last fifteen years, several presidents, including former President George W. Bush and current President Barack Obama, have promised a comprehensive immigration reform. While undocumented immigrants hoped to be included in such reform, these reform promises remain unfulfilled. In fact, the last reform in the U.S. immigration law was in 1986, when President Ronald Reagan signed the Immigration Reform and Control Act (IRCA), also known as the Simpson-Mazzoli Act. This legislation made it illegal to knowingly hire or recruit undocumented immigrants and required employers to verify their employees' immigration status. However, this legislation granted amnesty to certain undocumented immigrants residing continuously in the United States before January 1, 1982.

The terms *undocumented immigrants, unauthorized immigrants, and illegal aliens* refer to people who do not have the necessary documents allowing them to work and live in the U.S. Those opposing such immigrants typically use the adjective *illegal*, rather than *undocumented*. Some authors (Mortesen, 2009; Camarota, 2001; Glazer, 1995) use the term *illegal aliens*, supporting the view that entering a country without authorization is a Federal crime, and conclude that illegal immigration is not in the U.S.' best interest. Mortensen (2009) notes that being in the U.S. without documents is a criminal offense and that the euphemism *undocumented* should not be used because illegal immigrants commit such felonies as stealing identities, obtaining jobs illegitimately, and abusing social services. He, also, adds that illegal immigrants send their money to their country of origin, instead of spending it in the U.S.

According to The National Council of La Raza (2003), while the number of documented Latinos receiving welfare has declined dramatically since the Temporary Assistance for Needy Families program (TANF) was created, as part of the welfare reform in 1996, Hispanic women have tended to leave the rolls at a slower rate than their white and black counterparts, and Hispanic families have become a larger portion of immigrants on welfare. The lack of English-Spanish interpreters makes serving the Spanish-speaking population difficult. Because of their immigration status, many Latinos do not qualify for social services, including food stamps and social security checks. Even U.S. legal residents or green-card holders are no longer eligible for such services. In addition to this, Hernandez (2004), states that prior to the welfare reform, children in immigrant families were about as likely as, or only slightly more likely than, children in U.S.-born families to live in families receiving public assistance, particularly non-cash assistance. Most of the differences that existed reflected higher participation for first-generation children.

Anti-Immigration Arguments:

Some researchers (Mortensen, 2009; Borjas, 2001, Camarota, 2001) disregard the profitability of undocumented labor, the enormous contribution to the U.S. economy and diversity's positive impact on American culture. Instead, they focus on immigration's negative effect in the U.S. They state that undocumented Mexican immigrants have higher rates of poverty, possess little formal education, receive welfare, access public schools, and impose large fiscal costs on taxpayers. These researchers claim that illegal immigration results in job competition and decreased salaries for U.S. native workers. Camarota (2001), states that the more than ten million adult native-born U.S. workers that are not high school graduates face significant job competition from Mexican immigrants. Because the increase of unskilled immigrant workers has lowered the wages of U.S. native workers, the flow of immigrants adversely affects a social class that is already among the poorest in the United States. More than one-fourth of the native-born working poor lack a high school education, even those who are trying to move from welfare to work. The author recommends that policy makers (1) Develop programs for improving the work skills of legal Mexican immigrants to enable them to compete better in the U.S., and (2) Create policies reducing the number of unskilled legal and illegal immigrants entering the U.S. because of the negative economic impact they are having.

Other authors (Bacon, 2008; Chang, 2008; Chomsky, 2007), on the contrary, emphasize the value of immigrants in the U.S. The following section describes the contribution that these workers make and the mixed message that prevails about their right to be in this country.

Support for Undocumented Immigrants:

Research shows that the same workers that the U.S. uses as part of the workforce are considered disposable goods when they are not needed. According to Bacon (2008), several trade agreements between the U.S. and Latin America's countries, including the North America Free Trade Agreement (NAFTA), displaced workers who became an integral part of the U.S. economy, either undocumented or visa workers, who lived under conditions of virtual servitude. The same system that produces immigration criminalizes these workers labeling them as illegal immigrants and sending them home when they are not needed. Chang (2008) states, "The notion that immigrants can be treated as expendable commodities, to be used and expelled from the country or simply from any public concern, has guided immigration law and labor practice throughout U.S. history" (p. 93).

Several authors (Passel & Fix, 2001; Portes, 2006; Fukuyama, 2006) support the flow of undocumented Mexican immigrants and state that these immigrants strengthen the U.S. economy by filling jobs U.S. citizens refuse to do and tend to promote diversity and tolerance, both positive values welcomed in any society. These authors point that undocumented immigrants are the most vulnerable immigration group, struggling in terms of finances, education, and isolation, and the root of their hardship seems to be their immigration status. Recent researchers (Fix, Zimmerman, & Passel, 2001) include the terms *undocumented immigrants*, and refrain from using the term *illegal aliens*, avoiding terminology that reinforces the idea that undocumented immigrants are criminals, and disagreeing with the idea that staying in a country without documents is a crime. Understanding that several immigration issues remain unresolved, these authors support both, expanding the national discussion about integrating immigrants, and welcoming them without documentation.

Passel & Fix (2001), acknowledge immigration's impact in the U.S. They state that a national debate of immigration issues, including immigrants' socioeconomic and educational backgrounds is crucial, criticize a lack of legislation, and emphasize the need for an immigration reform The authors are particularly concerned about the level of integration and adaptation of new immigrants and their children. Regarding educational attainment, the authors state that immigrants have lower levels of education than natives, in fact, 32% of the foreign-born population aged 25-64 is not high school graduates versus only 11% of natives in the same age group.

While this book's goal is not to examine exhaustively the legal aspects of immigration, they cannot be ignored given the impact recommendations have on the possibility of an immigration reform. Undocumented Mexican immigrants are already here in this country and they are one of the more vulnerable groups of immigrants. They struggle not only with their financial situation but also with adjusting to a new country and trying to find a balance between their culture and the new country's values. Bacon (2008) states,

> But "illegal" also describes a social reality—inequality. Applied to immigrants, it has very little to do with the violation of a law or crossing a border. For centuries, there were no visas or "papers" needed in order to enter the United States, and anyone could walk across the border. It is still a minor civil violation to be in the country without documents. "Illegal" is all about social and political status. "Illegal" says society is divided into those who have rights and those who do not, those whose status and presence in the U.S. is legitimate and those whose status is illegitimate, those who are part of the community and those who are not. Yet those branded as illegal are part of the economic engine of this country (p. v).

Mexican Immigrant Women

Society has been defined as a group of people with varied interests that create conflicting forces. Freire (1970), states that these forces generate social tension and the more unequal a society is the more tension that society will have. As stated in this chapter, the study of immigration shows undocumented immigrant women as a powerless group with strong signs of detachment from the mainstream society, and who face severe hardships. Before analyzing the image of Mexican women, some concepts, to better understand societal power structures, must be explored. Johnson (1997), states that the crucial aspect to understand about patriarchy or any other kind of social system is that it is something where people participate. Johnson uses the popular game *Monopoly* as a metaphor for society. In society, as in the game, the participants follow specific routine patterns of feelings and behaviors. Advocating change, he says we have to think in a different way to promote changes in the dynamic of society. Although some groups in society, undoubtedly, have more power than others and make the rules for the *Monopoly*, we all constitute society; therefore, the way we think affects society's rules. Johnson, also, notes that the problem with the model of social life is that everything seems to be understood in terms of individuals. Everything begins and ends in individuals. The author coined the expression *something larger than ourselves*, referring to the social and institutional role. Rather than advocating an individualistic approach, Johnson thinks that organizations, schools, churches, and businesses shape individuals in different ways. Johnson, also, explores language's effect in society. Words like *patriarchy*, *racism*, or *oppression* create a counter-reaction in people who take those words personally as being against what is supposed to be their status quo or privileges.

According to McIntosh (1988), men are unwilling to accept their own privileges although they may accept that women are disadvantaged. Additionally, the study of machismo and feminism refers to issues related to power. Riger (1992) disagrees with the scientific methods used in social sciences and advocates a change in the paradigm. She understands the study of women as a product of social interaction, determined by socio-cultural, historical, and political contexts, rather than as a product of methodological procedures used in natural sciences. Gergen (1985), when analyzing social constructionism points four main points: (a) Social constructionism invites one to challenge the objective basis of conventional knowledge (including the fact that the observer modifies the object), (b) The understanding of the world is based in "social artifacts, products of historically situated interchanges among people" as a result of an active, cooperative enterprise of persons in relationships, (c) The rules for "what counts as what" are inherently ambiguous, continuously evolving, and free to vary," and (d) Forms of negotiated understanding play an important role in social life. Fiske (1993), states that stereotyping people is an effort to control them and as a category-based cognitive response to another person. She states that stereotyping operates in the service of control.

<u>Image of Mexican Women:</u>

The stereotypical image of Hispanic women shows them as docile, passive, and submissive to men. Based on this image, the role of women is to protect their families by being good wives and dedicated mothers, while disregarding their own desires and dreams. In his book *El Laberinto de la Soledad (The Labyrinto of Solitude)*, written in 1950, the well-known Mexican writer Octavio Paz (1914-1998) portrays Mexican and American cultures and describes Mexican women. Having lived in several countries including Spain, France, and the U.S., Paz describes Mexicans as solitaire and distrustful who have a strong sense of sacrifice and portrays Mexican women as submissive, passive, lacking determination, and obedient to their men's instincts. Paz (1950) illustrates his perception of Hispanic women with the following paragraph:

> Our Spanish-Arabic inheritance is only a partial explanation of this conduct. The Spanish attitude toward women is very simple. It is expressed quite brutally and concisely in these two sayings: "A woman's place is in the home, with a broken leg" and "Between a female saint and a male saint, a wall of mortared stone." Woman is a domesticated wild animal, lecherous and sinful from birth, who must be subdued with a stick and guided by the "reins of religion." Therefore Spaniards consider other women—especially those of a race or religion different from their own—to

be easy game. Mexicans consider woman to be a dark, secret and passive being. He does not attribute evil instincts to her; he even pretends that she does not have any. Or, to put it more exactly, her instincts are not her own but those of the species, because she is an incarnation of the life force, which is essentially impersonal. Thus it is impossible for her to have a personal, private life, for if she were to be herself if she were to be mistress of her own wishes, passions or whims-she would be unfaithful to herself (pp.36-37).

While Paz's description is very direct and even brutal, other authors analyze Mexican women's role in similar ways. For example, Quinones-Mayo & Dempsey (2005), state that given the increasing number of Hispanic women in the United States and their specific needs, social workers must empower these women, so they can participate in the mainstream society. They, also, explain that the values Hispanic women bring from their countries of origin are dictated by the belief in male superiority and dominance, popularized as *Machismo*, and legitimated through patriarchal social systems. Additionally, the authors in their article "Finding the Bicultural Balance: Immigrant Latino Mothers Raising 'American' Adolescents", include the term *Marianismo* to define the other side of machismo. They state that Latino families are hierarchical and the man is the authority in the family but the other side of that is the overprotection to women who are supposed to be submissive and obedient.

Following this approach, Gil & Vazquez (2002), analyze the huge dissonance that Mexican women experience when coming to the U.S. where the rules are different. The authors describe the concept of *Marianismo* as a backside of machismo. Women identify themselves with the Virgin Mary, have no sexual desire, and are pure and submissive to their parents and spouses. According to the authors, Hispanic women are expected to be nice, understanding, and pure like the Virgin Mary (from whom the term *Marianismo* comes). Undoubtedly, this concept resulted from the strong influence that Catholicism, the dominant religion in Mexico, has in the Hispanic culture. Although younger generations have questioned for decades the woman's role and the rules prevailing in the society, women are still struggling to be independent. Given these cultural images, when coming to the U.S., Mexican immigrant women find a big conflict between their culture and America's values. This conflict creates confusion, feelings of guilt, and strongly affects their sense of identity. The authors, psychotherapists based in New York, define the traditional roles of Hispanic women in a patriarchal society. Gil & Vazquez (2002) describe *The Ten Commandments of Marianismo* as follows:

1. Do not forget the place of the woman
2. Do not give up your traditions
3. Do not be an old maid, independent, or have your own opinions
4. Do not put your needs first
5. Do not wish anything but to be a house wife
6. Do not forget sex is to make babies, not pleasure
7. Do not be unhappy with your man, no matter what he does to you
8. Do not ask for help
9. Do not discuss your personal problems outside the house
10. Do not change. (p. 25)

Women in the Hispanic culture are to be devoted supporters of their husband and children. In the traditional Hispanic family, independence is not considered a value. Instead the family and accomplishments within the family unit are highly valued. Women are not supposed to put their needs first, behavior that is seen as selfishness, rather than autonomy and self-determination. On the contrary, they are to be people pleasers who postpone their own dreams for the family's well-being. Furthermore, they are not to discuss private issues in public or with anyone outside the family. This may explain in part why victims of domestic violence have difficulty seeking help because of feelings of shame and dishonor and a misplaced loyalty to their abusive husbands. Undoubtedly, economic factors condition these women to remain submissive.

Compounding this problem, their educational opportunities are limited, their social class determined their chances to attain formal education, and helped perpetuate their dependency on men. Most of these women see marriage as an *escape* from their parents' house. In the literature, the Latino family has been represented, for the most part, as a homogeneous group with a patriarchal structure in which the man is head of the household and the women and children have a more submissive role.

The stress on cultural sameness overlooks a great variety of influences among Latin American nations—ethnic, racial, historical and cultural variables. Authors use interchangeably the words *Hispanics* and *Latinos*, which is a generalization that labels a group of people from different countries and cultures, disregarding their particular background and identities. Mexican mothers may fit in the *Latino* or *Hispanic* stereotype as well as a person born in Spain or Cuba, however, disregarding all the differences that each culture group offers. The use of these labels, *Hispanics or Latinos*, was created to include any person whose native language is Spanish regardless of their culture of origin. Wells (1968), states that even though Latinos show dissimilarities about their values from country to country, they share a common matrix of the Latino experience. Quinones-Mayo & Dempsey (2005), note that although influenced by more than 100 years of U.S. control, Puerto Rico has maintained a history of assertive feminism, dating back to the Taino Indian experience. However, countries of the southern cone, such as Argentina and Chile, show a markedly heavier Western European influence that has altered some traditional Spanish cultural beliefs.

The role of women, or what others expect from them, is a social construction varying from culture to culture. In other words, the role of women reflects the society's beliefs and values. For instance, a society that values submission and virginity will reward those behaviors, whereas a society that emphasizes independency and individualism will reward these values. Several researchers, such as Berger & Luckmann (1966), support the idea that reality is socially constructed.

The process of understanding is not automatically driven by the forces of nature, but is the result of an active, cooperative enterprise of the persons in relationship. According to Berger & Luckmann, the specific contents that are internalized in primary socialization vary, of course, from society to society. The authors state that reality is a quality appertaining to phenomena that we recognize as having a being independent of our own volition (we cannot "wish them away"). Therefore, the reality erupts in our lives beyond our desire and beyond any preconception we have about reality. According to the authors, knowledge is the certainty that phenomena are real and that they possess specific characteristics. However, the interpretation of that reality is a social construction and changes from context to context. In other words, sociology of knowledge will have to deal not only with the empirical variety of "knowledge" in human societies, but also with the process by which any body of knowledge comes to be socially established as *reality*.

Immigrant Mexican Women: Double Disadvantage

Quinones-Mayo & Dempsey (2005) emphasize that parents show differences in rearing children based on their parental belief systems. Mexican immigrant families living and raising adolescents in the U.S. exhibit a particular belief system based on their previous educational background, life experiences, traditions, and values. The authors states that the helping professions need to re-evaluate how they deliver services to the growing number of newcomers. The growth of immigration challenges the social work profession to first explore the complex matrix of diversity in a rapidly changing world of broken borders and then find new ways of delivering services to populations in need. Mexican mothers face a complicated task disciplining their high school children. They struggle not only with the conflicts associated with this difficult stage of adolescence, such as consolidating their identity, questioning parental values and house rules, but also with the dissonances between the Mexican and American cultures. While Mexican mothers try to preserve their traditions, adolescents imitate their peers as a way to be accepted in the new society.

Greenfield, Trumbull, Keller, Rothstein-Fisch, Suzuki, & Quiroz (2006) indicate that the learning process varies substantially across different cultures. Undoubtedly, the differences between the Mexican and American cultures tremendously affect their adaptation process. Also, the school system is part of a culture. Therefore, the school beliefs and values will determine the quality of the teaching/learning process. According to Greenfield et all (2006),

> In recent years, a body of evidence has cohered around a unifying and powerful way to tie together cultural conceptions of learning and development. With origins from developmental psychology (Greenfield & Brunner, 1966) and anthropology (Whiting & Whiting, 1973), this parsimonious theory posits two idealized developmental pathways: one emphasizing individual identity, independence, self-fulfillment, and standing out. The other emphasizing group identity, interdependence, social responsibility, and fitting in. (p. 676)

While the first pathway is termed *individualistic*, the latter is identified as *collectivistic* or *sociocentric*. Individualistic cultures emphasize and value independence, while collectivistic cultures stress the success of the group as a whole. However, cultures are not purely individualistic or collectivistic, but exhibit elements of both—particularly when cultures encounter one other. Mexican immigrants were raised in a collectivistic culture but live in an individualistic one. Therefore, their beliefs and values suffer from a profound transformation or at least a modification in adapting to a new culture. Undocumented immigrant mothers come from poor families with little opportunity for educational advancement. Hence, they are likely to exhibit highly collectivistic values.

Payne (2005), states that social work is socially constructed through interactions with clients. They become defined as clients by social processes, and social workers are actors defined by social forces and the social context. To better deliver services and meet needs, those working with undocumented families must become familiar with their cultural values—that can be in conflict with American values at times. One of the main problems Mexican mothers complain about is that social workers empower children by advising them to express themselves, thus denigrating parental authority. Quinones-Mayo & Dempsey (2005) added that Latino mothers express feelings of being betrayed by the professionals from whom they seek help. Immigrant children are the connection between their parents' values and American values. However, teaching and advising parents about parenting skills or about developing alternative ways of discipline, requires understanding the parents' culture and children-rearing tradition.

Education of Immigrant Children

Children of undocumented immigrants represent an important part of the nation's future labor force. According to Valdivieso & Siobhan (1992), "One quarter of all Hispanic families are poor by federal guidelines; and therefore, many Hispanic children are likely to live below the poverty line. In 1990, census data revealed that 38% of Hispanic children, compared to 44% of African-American children and 15% of white children, lived in families with incomes below the official poverty line" (p.20). Fortuny, Capps, Simms, & Chaudry (2009), state that children of immigrants deserve special attention because they face many universal risks to their well-being, such as lower parental education and family incomes, and are also adversely affected by factors unique to immigration, such as lack of both parental citizenship and English proficiency. Hernandez (2004) agrees that undocumented immigrants have been neglected and that clear and efficient policies are needed to better serve undocumented immigrant families. He summarizes the circumstances of immigrants' children:

(a) Children in immigrant families are much less likely than children in native-born families to have only one parent in the home, and they are nearly twice as likely as those in native-born families to be living with grandparents, other relatives, and non-relatives.

(b) Parental educational attainment is perhaps the most central feature of family circumstances relevant to overall child well-being and development, regardless of race/ethnicity or immigrant origins.

(c) Children in immigrant families were only slightly less likely than children in native-born families to have a father who worked during the past year, but many of their fathers worked less than full-time year-round.

(d) Official poverty rates for children in immigrant families are substantially higher than for children in native-born families 21% versus 14% (p.22).

In addition to the socioeconomic factors describe above, these children struggle with assimilation and other social issues. Striving to become accepted by their mainstream peers, these students often shun their primary language or dialect and cultural practices to become assimilated into mainstream society. While liberal multiculturalism is promoted in the classroom, current educational practices promote quick assimilation. Balderrama & Diaz-Rico (2006), note that educators working with immigrant children should consider research indicating that immigrant students who preserve both cultures show better results integrating into the new culture. Furthermore, teachers should show respect and curiosity for their immigrant students' cultures.

School Failure:

School failure is a complex problem that includes students' socioeconomic status, parents' educational attainment, schools' literacy programs, and curriculum. Research shows that a high percentage of children of immigrants are failing in school. According to Camarota (2001), almost two-thirds of adult Mexican immigrants have not completed high school, compared to fewer than one in ten Native Americans. Mexican immigrants now account for 22% of all high school dropouts in the labor force. The author added, "The lower educational attainment of

Mexican immigrants appears to persist across generations. The high school dropout rates of native-born Mexican-Americans (both second and third generation) are two and a half times that of other natives. As a result, native-born Mexican Americans lag far behind other natives in income, welfare use, and other measures of socio-economic well being" (p.7). While noting that research in educational inequalities among minority students is vast, Valencia, Valenzuela, Sloan & Foley (2001) seek specific answers from schools about excluding disadvantaged students from their right to equal educational opportunities.

Because many immigrants lack the education and English skills to understand the school and legal systems' rules (some of which are not explicit), their adjustment to a new culture is seriously limited. One of the main issues with immigrant children is truancy. According to the Tennessee Department of Education, the school system requires 180 days of classroom instruction. Students' parents or guardians must be given written notice each time a student misses five unexcused school days. However, because of the immigrant parents' unawareness of the laws, lack of English skills and inability to communicate with school authorities, many immigrant children enter state custody because of truancy. Although Mexico's school system includes mandatory classes, truant children are not removed from their homes, and parents do not go to jail. Therefore, the differences between the American and Mexican educational systems create confusion.

In addition to that, a sizable body of research (Freire, 1970; Valencia & Black, 2002) supports the idea that school failure is a social phenomenon and cannot be fixed by the school. Valencia states that school failure can be fully understood only when analyzed in the broadest political, economic, and cultural contexts. Macro policies establish the boundaries of possibilities. Freire (1970), on the other hand, states that education is a tool for social change but requires the whole society's participation. Dudley-Marling (2004) notes that the idea that school is responsible for school failure and can fix this problem overestimates the educational system's power disregarding other factors, such as socioeconomic conditions. The design of technical solutions focused on one aspect of education shows a limited understanding of this complex phenomenon.

English as a Second Language (ESL):

One of the main obstacles in adapting to the new country is the language barrier. Unfortunately, socio-economic conditions, the need to survive in the U.S., and the lack of time make acquiring a new language a complicated goal that some of the immigrants never accomplish. This difficulty exists despite the fact that several organizations, including churches and social agencies, offer free English classes. Immigrant mothers often work full-time jobs and have no time to attend English classes. In addition, some of these mothers are illiterate in their native language, making the acquisition of English even more unattainable.

Immigrant children, on the other hand, must be English proficient to succeed in school. ESL teaching approaches are an important area in the development of programs for immigrant students. According to the Tennessee Department of Education, ESL students are to receive 45 minutes of ESL classes twice a week to become proficient in English. However, ESL teachers face several problems. According to Miller & Endo (2004), teachers must consider several factors in designing ESL classes: (1) Reducing the cognitive load by selecting activities that allow students to include their previous knowledge (fragmentation in educational background delays acquisition of a second language), (2) Evaluating teaching strategies and approaches, which affect the learning experience. Teachers need to ensure that ESL students feel comfortable in the new environment, understand the school's hidden rules, and feel free to interact with other classmates by providing clear directions and understanding students individually. For example, in some countries, the role of the teacher is unquestioned and venerated. ESL students may feel uncomfortable asking a question or approaching their teacher informally. An inexperienced teacher can interpret these behaviors as being shy or unmotivated instead of resulting from cultural issues, (3) Reducing the cultural load. The author notes that reducing the cultural load for immigrant students can make learning a more positive experience. In addition, teachers must show respect for immigrant students, not judgment, by building personal relationships with their students and their families and their culture. (4) Reducing the language load. Using unfamiliar and sophisticated words creates anxiety. The author suggests using strategies to lower the language load. For example, the teacher can rewrite texts using simpler terms so students can understand them easily, and provide several sources that include different levels of linguistic difficulty including native language with English, and (5) Uniting parents and teachers as a team (p. 789).

Another important suggestion Miller & Endo make is including the native language with English. This inclusion is the topic of an old debate in acquiring a second language. While some authors emphasize using English exclusively, others believe the connection between the native language and English is greatly beneficial to immigrant students. Finally, Miller & Endo (2004) identify four important steps parents and teachers should take together:

(a) Emphasize the importance of learning the native language in addition to English,
(b) Understand the emotional aspect that immigrant students face,
(c) Monitor the negative impact of negative forces in the immigrant child's life,
(d) Encourage participation in community activities providing a sense of belonging and a great opportunity for social interaction, and
(e) Encourage parents to visit classrooms and participate in school activities.

According to Miller & Endo (2004), three main issues must be considered in designing ESL teaching methods. (1) The use of the first language as crucial in the *making meaning* in the acquisition of the second language, (2) The acceptance of the culture that each student brings to emphasize the idea that *all cultures are equally valuable*, and (3) The contribution that these students make to the new culture is unique and central. Multicultural classes offer big advantages over more uniform classes. High-diversity classes are a win-win situation for native English students and immigrant children.

According to Balderrama & Diaz-Rico (2006), a myriad of teachers are committed to providing a safe learning environment in which values like respect, equity, and justice are emphasized despite the learning approaches to which these teachers may adhere. In addition, teachers are in charge of transmitting cultural values. Teachers must promote the idea that all languages are created equal, and students' linguistic repertories are different, their dialects should be honored, respected, and used as a resource toward their acquisition of English. Roessingh (2006), on the other hand, emphasizes the need of up-to-date programs to meet the student's needs. He points that the ever-increasing number of immigrant students indicates the need to reconsider the efficacy of current teaching methods.

ESL teachers deal with high-diversity classes. They need to develop specific teaching approaches to successfully engage their students in acquiring a second language. Another important aspect in the study of ESL teaching programs is multicultural or high-diversity classes. High-diversity within a population refers to that population's practices, traditions, customs, values, and beliefs. Hanley (1999) describes each culture as being like an iceberg: while some elements are on the surface—for example dress, cooking, games,—other deep elements remain hidden, such as patterns of relationships, concepts of justice, social responsibility, and friendship. Nieto (2002), points out that multicultural education is needed as part of new educational plans to serve immigrant students. She states,

> Multicultural education is a process of comprehensive
> school reform and basic education for all students.

> It challenges and rejects racism and other forms of discrimination in schools and society and accepts and affirms the pluralism (ethnic, racial, linguistic, religious, economic, and gender among others) that students, their communities, and teachers reflect. (pp. 29-30).

Teachers are the transmitters of cultural values. They are the mediators between a culture and students, facilitating the learning process. According to Roessingh (2006), in ESL settings, perhaps more than in any other teaching and learning context, the learner must attach personal meaning. The new concepts that ESL students acquire, are related, integrated, assimilated, and stored, but their first language operates as a pivot in the learning process. Part of this "making meaning" refers to multicultural education. When a teacher leads a class with 30 students who speak ESL and come from different countries, environments, cultures, "making meaning" becomes essential.

The No Child Left Behind Act (NCLB):

One of the attempts to solve school failure was the *No Child Left Behind* (NCLB) Act of 2001, which emphasizes that the school is responsible for its failure, and must take corrective actions. However, during the implementation of the NCLB, school dropouts have not decreased, at least among Hispanic immigrant students. The NCLB reauthorized the Elementary and Secondary Education Act (ESEA). The NCLB Act includes four main principles: (a) Accountability for results, (b) Increased number of choices for parents, (c) Greater local control and flexibility, and (d) Emphasis on scientific research. NCLB supports the accountability of Title I, federally funded programs that support high-poverty schools with low-achieving students. The act requires states to implement statewide accountability systems covering all public schools. These systems, based on state standards in reading and mathematics for all groups, should include analysis of poverty, race, ethnicity, disability, and limited English proficiency to ensure that no group is "left behind."

According to Bullough (2002), the NCLB Act has received several criticisms. Unlike the traditional view that the school can correct its failure, other theories suggest that school failure is the result of different factors in the whole society, and the school just reflects those factors. In his article "Thoughts on Teacher Education in the USA," Bullough notes that Americans have a strong tendency to think that every social problem is an educational problem and can be fixed by the school instead of acknowledging economic inequalities. In fact, the NCLB Act emphasizes the role of the school, the teachers' background or credentials, and the number of hours ESL students receive, but says nothing about the social environment in which these immigrant children are immersed. For example, one of the main problems that ESL teachers face is lack of family support. Consequently, teachers must be committed to engage parents in school activities and make every effort to include them in the school system.

Other authors, Lenz (2002), on the contrary, when criticizing the NCLB Act, focus on schools, teachers, and curriculum while disregarding socioeconomic conditions. The author states that school failure is caused by the principals' and teachers' lack of training to meet low-income children's needs. She adds that the NCLB Act will not be effective until this issue is addressed. The NCLB act is based on the promise that all children will receive education. This promise sounds powerful but is unrealistic. Identifying the causes of school failure and developing realistic plans include a comprehensive and integral study of the schools and the whole society. A complete analysis of the NCLB Act is beyond this book's purpose. However, the Act has done little if anything to help immigrant students. When coming to the U.S., Mexican-born students have the extra burden of the language barrier. Although schools must provide ESL classes, the language gap persists, leaving students behind and unable to meet the school expectations.

Besides the functional obstacles, such as lack of time, money, or other resources to be able to provide ESL classes, the NCLB does not address the social challenges that ESL teachers face everyday with immigrant children.

Legislation for ESL Students in Tennessee (NCLB):

The growing immigrant population in the U.S. has resulted in revised legislation for immigrant children. According to the NCLB, ESL is a program for delivering services to students whose primary language is not English. In Tennessee, ESL services are primarily delivered by pulling students out of the regular classroom, providing English instruction at their ability level, and then returning them to the classroom. Seivers & McCargar (2005) describe Title III in the NCLB,

> The Language Instruction for Limited English Proficient and Immigrant Students program, assists school districts in teaching English to students who are limited in English proficiency and in helping these students meet the same challenging state standards required of all students. Title III consolidates the 13 current bilingual and immigrant education programs into a State formula program and significantly increases flexibility and accountability (p.52).

The main changes in the NCLB are the following: (1) Requires that teachers be certified as English language proficient, (2) Requires that curricula be demonstrated to be effective, (3) Provides discretion over instructional methods, (4) Targets funds to the classroom, (5) Establishes annual achievement objectives for limited English proficient students, (6) Sees English language proficiency as the objective, (7) Requires reading and language arts assessments of children in English, (8) Enforces accountability requirements: States must hold subgrantees accountable for making adequate yearly progress, and (9) Notifying parents about program placements.

Additionally, the NCLB changes in accountability are the following: (a) States must establish annual achievement objectives for limited English proficient students that are related to gains in English proficiency and meeting challenging State academic standards and that are aligned with Title I achievement standards and (b) States must assure that subgrantees will comply with the Title I requirement to annually assess, in English, children who have been in the U.S. for three or more consecutive years. States must hold subgrantees accountable for making adequate yearly progress as described in Title I and for meeting all annual achievement objectives.

Several researchers such as Garret & Holcomb (2005) note that the number of immigrant students with limited English ability, commonly referred to as English Limited Learners (ELLs), enrolled in schools throughout the United States is growing rapidly. Schools are obligated to take immigrant students regardless of their immigration status. According to the Federal law, undocumented students are to receive education until age eighteen regardless of their immigration status. English language skills as a prerequisite for classes and for immigration in general have brought some controversy. Gunderson (2000), states that the expectation that all immigrant students will be proficient in English seems unrealistic.

Parental Involvement

A sizable body of research (Driessen, Frederik, & Sleegers, 20005; Greenberg, 2000; Henderson & Mapp, 2002; Okagaki & Sternberg, 1993; Ramirez, 2003; Sartor & Youniss, 2002; Valencia & Black, 2002) shows that parental involvement is crucial for students' academic success. Students with parents actively involved are more likely to earn high grades and test scores, enroll in higher-level programs, have a more positive attitude toward school, and set higher goals. Additionally, Sconyers (1996) notes that increasing the relationship between the school and parents, is critical for improving the students' performance, especially for disadvantaged groups, such as ethnic minority and low socio-economic students. The author adds that parents want schools to be involved in the lives of their children and the community in which they live. However, the author says that the problem is that parents see the child as a whole, while schools have traditionally been more focused on intellectual development.

Yet, many native-born parents struggle with school participation either because they struggled themselves as students, or they work long hours and cannot attend parent-teacher conferences, or they do not feel comfortable going to their children's school. However, many immigrants face an even greater obstacle to parental involvement, their lack of understanding the educational system, including its legalities, represents a tremendous obstacle. According to Valdivieso & Siobhan (1992), the parents' educational attainment—either for native-born or immigrant parents—plays a crucial role in the students' school performance. Urrieta & Quach (2000), state that the U.S. educational system lacks the resources to address immigration issues. Therefore, educational issues involving language minority students and students of color continue to cause much debate and controversy.

Freire (1970) states that education is a political phenomenon, intimately related to personal and collective experience and defines education as a process for conscientization, social change, and liberation. Contrary to the traditional model of education in which teachers have a superior status and transmit knowledge that students receive passively, Freire's method is based on the belief that education is a social experience. Therefore, dialogue is used as a tool in the teaching/learning process and parents are included in this process. Freire's model offers an excellent tool to improve parental involvement and engage parents in their children's educational process. Additionally, Freire criticizes the traditional model based on lectures, which reflects the societal dynamics of domination and oppression. Instead, Freire's theory uses learning as a process to perceive social, political, and economic contradictions, developing a critical understanding of reality, whereby individuals can take action against the oppressive elements of their reality.

The school system includes programs, content, methods, and objectives that vary from society to society. Therefore, the literacy process must be understood contextually because it occurs under specific political conditions within given contexts. Undocumented immigrants are unfamiliar with the school rules in the U.S. They are unaware of the school programs, content, and objectives. Even though the integration of these workers exceeds the school participation, the school is to be an agent of change and participation to include these parents in the school life. In Freire's model, school failure is defined as a social construction because schools reflect a society's cultural values. For instance, if a society is oppressive, schools will be oppressive; if a society promotes dialogue and equal participation, schools will do so. Therefore, Freire argues that preventing school failure should be based on plans that include social variables as an essential part of the problem.

CHAPTER THREE

RESEARCH METHODS

To seek the essence of perception is to declare that perception is, not presumed true, but defined as access to truth.
Merleau-Ponty

The research question for this book is "What are the experiences of undocumented Mexican mothers of high school students living in the U.S. who received social services?" Ten undocumented Mexican mothers of high school students, whom I assisted during my years working as a bilingual therapist at a social service agency, were selected to participate in this research. Participants had to meet specific requirements to qualify for this study: (1) Undocumented Mexican immigrants, (2) Mexican mothers, (3) Having children in high school, (4) Having a minimum of five years living in the U.S., and (5) Recipients of social services due to their children's problems.

Selecting Participants

This section explains how participants were selected and why these requirements were important for this research.

(1) <u>Undocumented Mexican immigrants</u>: During my years working with undocumented families, I learned that most of these immigrants had serious financial problems. Because of their immigration status, they did not qualify for social services such as food stamps, social security, and health insurance. One of the areas that this research explores is the financial limitations that undocumented immigrants face in the U.S.

(2) <u>Mexican Mothers</u>: Traditionally, in the Hispanic culture, the role of mothers is related to care, advice, and protection of their families, husband and children. Commonly, the mother is the one who stays at home, or even if she works, she is the one who takes care of the children. Fathers take care of their children but their beliefs, values, and roles are different. They are traditionally the providers, the ones who go to work and bring the money to support their families. While the participants in this study held this role as mothers in Mexico, they were living in the U.S. where their role was seen quite differently by the mainstream society.

(3) <u>Mothers of High School Students</u>: The third requirement for these participants was that these mothers had to have children in high school. A common stereotype about Hispanic families is that they do not value education. This book explored the experiences of these mothers raising their children and their beliefs and expectations about education. During my years working with undocumented immigrants, mothers have shared feelings of frustration. They seemed to be unable to understand the school system, and had major problems communicating with school authorities. One of the main objectives of this book was to explore in depth the experience of these mothers, their relationship with the school system, and their beliefs and expectations for their children.

(4) <u>Years lived in the U.S.</u>: The fourth requirement was the time they lived in the U.S. The study was oriented to mothers who have spent at least five years in the U.S. which is enough time to allow them to settle or at least have some meaningful and relevant experiences in the new country.

(5) <u>Social Services</u>: The last requirement was that these mothers received or were receiving social services at the time of the interview. All participants were involved with DCS either before or at the time of the interview. They

received services through a social service agency that assisted families facing crisis, through its home based program, with the overall purpose of preserving the family unit. This home based program was designed to serve males and females children of any age (0-18 years), who were in immediate risk of coming into state custody and/or provide reunification services where the initial adjustment to home or foster home was in jeopardy due to the explosive behavioral and/or emotional nature of the youth. Adolescents currently at-risk with the juvenile justice system for status offenses were also eligible for this service. The main reasons were truancy, domestic violence, substance abuse, vandalism, among others. This book intended to identify the main problems that made DCS get involved with these families, the resources that these mothers implemented to overcome these problems, and the specific help these families received.

Beside the requirements explained above, participants shared several characteristics that resulted in a fairly homogeneous group. All participants were monolingual (Spanish) with the exception of one participant whose first language was a native Mexican dialect (Tarasco) and spoke limited Spanish. All participants had little formal education; elementary education or less. Only one mother finished high school. Two participants reported they were illiterate in their own language. All participants were unskilled workers who had jobs in restaurants, factories, or landscaping. The following section describes the site and participants included in this research.

Site and Participants

As stated in Chapter One, I worked as a bilingual therapist at a contracted service provider for DCS. I worked with American and Hispanic families. Most of these Hispanic families were undocumented Mexican immigrants with Mexican-born and/or U.S.-born high school students. Children involved with DCS were unsuccessful in school, made poor grades, missed several school days, had discipline problems, but most of all, these students did not seem to see school as a valuable tool to access the labor market, attain advanced education, or improve their integration level in the U.S. Some of the more common problems that these children presented were mental health and substance abuse problems, truancy, and domestic violence. Services were provided at their homes. Mothers, on the other hand, faced similar problems in their relationship with the school and the community in general. They did not have a successful experience in school as students. Most of them had little or no formal education. They did not speak English and were not integrated in the mainstream community since they could not communicate in English. Compounding this problem, some schools did not have interpreters available to better facilitate the interaction between the students' parents and the school staff.

Meeting with the Participants

At the time I started the interview process, I was working at an alternative school as a therapist, so I no longer had the daily contact either by phone or in person that I previously had with these mothers. After attempting to reach them by phone, I realized most of the phones had been disconnected. Therefore, I decided the best way to reach the participants was to drive to their homes during the day. Some of these mothers were not at home when I visited them, so I left polite notes with my name and phone number at their front doors. They, in turn, called me to schedule an appointment. As soon as I saw them again, I realized our relationship, including the trust and connection we had previously established, was still intact. Although each participant interviewed had a unique history, distinctive qualities, personalities, and individual experiences, they shared some common characteristics as reflected in Table 1 (page 46).

Introduction of Participants

Maria

Maria moved from Toluca, Mexico to the U.S. in 1995. Her husband came to the U.S. by himself in 1992. Then she came, leaving her four-year-old son in Mexico with his paternal grandparents for four years. She was a dedicated married mother of three children (ages 19, 12, and 3). Her two younger daughters were born in the U.S. Maria was a stay at home mother. She spent her day doing housework and taking care of her children. She was highly compliant during treatment, returning phone calls, attending all appointments at home, school, or DCS. She, also, was very connected to her children's needs and was very upset when things did not go well. I was assigned to work with her oldest son who had problems at school. He remained in Mexico until the age of eight when the paternal grandparents brought him to the U.S. This situation caused several problems in her son's life and the family unit. He became oppositional and defiant and told his parents that they did not love him because he was not American like his sisters. He started having problems in school, including smoking marijuana, and then was expelled for possessing a weapon in school. Although he has been in foster care for more than a year, Maria hoped to have him back home within the next few months. Maria did not speak English and was unemployed, but babysat some children in the neighborhood a couple of days a week.

Carmen

Carmen was a quiet mother from Mexico. She moved to California in 1980 and lived there until 2004. Then she moved to the southeast area of the U.S. She lived with her husband, who was Mexican, and their two children (ages 18 and 17), who were born in the U.S. She worked full time in a factory. She reported she did not speak English. During the interview, she was very kind and talkative. Struggling with her daughter's health problems, she said that her daughter suffered from depression, high blood pressure, and diabetes, since the family left California. I met this family two years ago when her daughter was involved with DCS. She was truant at school at that time due to her health problems. Fortunately, Carmen reported that her daughter would graduate from high school at the end of this year. However, Carmen shared her frustration about this situation and reported that her daughter was still very sick. She said she did not know what to do to help her. Carmen reported she was not able to work in California due to her immigration status. She said that situation changed after moving to the southeast area. She said she was content about her financial achievements, including buying a house and being economically stable.

Laura

A very kind and active woman, Laura came from Mexico to the U.S. in 2000. She said she had five children with three different men who lived with her at times. The children were 25, 24, 22, 19, and 15 years of age. All of her children were born in Mexico. Laura lived with three of her children. Her oldest son remained in Mexico and her 19 year old daughter lived with her boyfriend and their child. Laura reported she struggled a lot with her nineteen-year-old daughter when she was in high school. Her daughter, suffered from depression, had substance abuse problems, and was truant from school. During these difficult years, her daughter was charged with possession of cocaine, possession of a weapon, and physical assault. She was not compliant during treatment, violated her probation several times, cancelled appointments regularly, failed numerous drug tests, and ran away several times. The last time, the daughter ran away to Mexico, and stayed there for a year. Laura said she did not know what to do about the situation. During the interview, Laura said that her daughter was doing fine, living with her boyfriend and their one-year-old baby, but her youngest daughter, who was fifteen, was acting like her older sister. Laura reported she was afraid that her younger daughter was going to do the same things that her older sister did. Laura said she did not speak English and was unemployed. Although her older son and older daughter helped her financially, she was very worried about her economic situation.

Guadalupe

Guadalupe was a very polite middle-aged woman, who has lived in the U.S. since 2004. She was married and the mother of three children who were born in Mexico and were 22, 15, and 8 years of age. She stated that her husband has been deported three times. The first time, he was driving under the influence when the police stopped him. She reported she did not speak English and worked full time at a restaurant. Guadalupe said she was devastated the first time that her husband was deported. He was sent to prison in the U.S. for several months. She said she did not know what to do. However, she said she got a job relatively quickly, paid her bills, and was able to move forward. Unfortunately, her middle daughter had serious health problems; she suffered from epilepsy and had a stroke when she was one year old, leaving her with some neurological damage. As a result, her daughter had serious behavioral problems in school, including being aggressive and hitting her classmates. Guadalupe reported that her daughter received special education services. When she was asked about this she said she did not know why her daughter was in special education classes. Guadalupe said that her daughter has made great progress at school and at home with the help of her family, doctors, and state-provided health insurance.

Barbara

A married mother of three children (ages 22, 18, and 15). Barbara moved from Guanajuato, Mexico to California in 1989 with her husband and her oldest son. Her two younger children were born in the U.S. The family moved to the southeast part of the U.S. in 2000. Barbara said she did not speak English and worked in a factory. She said she had always worked in the U.S. During the interview she said she did not work in Mexico but here in the U.S. women have to work to support their families with their husbands. She seemed very depressed during the interview. She reported she was in an abusive relationship with her husband. Barbara said that her experience with her two younger children, who were born in the U.S., was "the saddest thing that happened to her in her whole life." She said that her problems started three years ago, when her daughter was raped at the age of fifteen, and no one helped her because she was Hispanic. Three years later, her daughter became pregnant and dropped out of high school. Barbara said she had other plans for her daughter; she would have loved for her to have been married before she was pregnant. In addition to that, Barbara reported that her fifteen year old son has been incarcerated since March 2009 and will be in prison until the end of this year for attempted robbery and possession of marijuana and paraphernalia in the street. In contrast, she stated that her older son, who was born in Mexico and did not have the privileges that her younger children had, was a wonderful kid and did not cause her any problems.

Rosa

Rosa was a widowed mother of six children. She has been widowed since 2000. Three of her children were diagnosed with epilepsy and died at a very young age. Rosa lived with her three daughters (ages 15, 14, and 12) and her four-year-old grandson whose mother died last year from epilepsy. Rosa said she has been married twice. Her first husband was an alcoholic, and her second husband was murdered in the U.S. She reported she did not know why her husband was murdered. She said she was with her husband at a store buying some groceries when a man came over and shot him. The case was closed last year and the murderer has not been prosecuted. Rosa reported she was currently unemployed. She lived in a public housing apartment. She received some financial help from the State. Her daughters were U.S. citizens and qualified for public housing and food stamps. Rosa said she did not want to remarry because her daughters were her life. She said, "You never know what is going to happen." Despite the tragedies she faced in her life, during the interview, she seemed very quiet and peaceful. She did not show any signs of anger. She seemed resigned and reconciled with her past. Rosa was the only participant who spoke a native Mexican dialect (Tarasco) as a first language. She spoke limited Spanish. She said she did not speak English. She reported that her daughters, who spoke English and Spanish, helped her whenever she needed to communicate with English-speaking people.

Leticia

Leticia was a very pleasant young mother, who has lived in the U.S. since 1999. She had three children (ages 19, 10, and 3). Her oldest son was born in Mexico and her two younger sons were born in the U.S. She reported she owned a business with her husband. She said she was raped by her older sister's husband and became pregnant at the age of fifteen. Part of her family blamed her for that incident; her sister has never spoken with her again. However, her parents supported her and helped her raise her oldest son. Then she came to the U.S., met her husband, and had two more children. I met this family six years ago. Her son was involved with DCS for truancy. He was in counseling for several months and made great progress. However, when the case was closed he ran away to Mexico. Leticia said she struggled a lot with her oldest son, who had serious problems in school and finally dropped out of high school. He refused to take the General Education Diploma (GED) test to obtain a high school diploma. Although she wanted him to finish school, he never did. She said he moved in with his girlfriend and the couple was expecting a baby. Leticia said she was fine with that situation but regretted that her son did not finish school. She said she did not want to be in that situation again. She said she was very dedicated to her middle son and wanted him to be successful in school and in life.

Mariana

Mariana was a kind and shy young mother, who came from Queretaro, Mexico to the U.S. in 2000. Working full time to support her family, she lived with her husband, three children (ages 16, 15, and 6) and two granddaughters. Her oldest daughter was raped at the ages of twelve and fourteen. Her daughter had two children with the same sex offender. Mariana was illiterate. She reported she did not finish elementary school in Mexico. She said she did not feel comfortable receiving social workers or therapists because that involved paperwork and she could not read. Mariana did not speak English. She stated that her oldest daughter translated for her and her husband.

She worked at a restaurant and reported, "She did not need to speak English to understand what the manager said." She said she understood what people said in English but "She could not talk". She seemed very submissive to her husband and afraid to talk during the interviews. For example, during my years working with this family, I observed that every time I asked her a question, she looked down, looked at her husband, and he responded to me. According to Mariana, a cousin raped her daughter; but the story seemed very confusing. She said she called the police to file a report but the cousin ran away to Mexico. Two years later, he returned to the U.S. and raped her daughter again. I met the family seven years ago. Mariana was very concerned about her immigration status. I explained to her that I was there to help regardless of her immigration status in this country. Mariana said she was very afraid when her daughter was pregnant. She thought she was going to be deported for being undocumented. The case was open for more than a year. It took months to build a relationship with this family but during the last months she seemed more comfortable talking about her family problems.

Teresa

Teresa was an energetic mother of six children (ages 19, 17, 15, 14, 12, and 10). She was separated at the time of the interview. She stated that her husband had problems with alcohol and she asked him to leave the house. She said he was an alcoholic since she met him. She reported she wanted to get divorced but did not know how to do that and did not have the money to hire a lawyer. Unemployed, Teresa did not speak English. She said she struggled a lot with her oldest son, who had serious behavioral problems and was expelled from high school. Afterwards, he took the GED and obtained a high school diploma. Rarely communicating with the school, she remembered being at the school just a few times with her sister-in-law, who spoke English. Teresa reported she did not understand the school rules. She said that her son was expelled for DUI (Driving under the influence of a substance). However, she said that her son did not drive. He had a bottle of alcohol (moonshine) in the school. When asked about that event, she said the school staff explained to her but she did not understand. She said the school did not provide interpreters. Despite her struggle, she seemed content with her children, remained hopeful about her life, and hoped that each of her children will marry a good person and have a family.

Juana

A nice woman, mother of three children (ages 19, 11, and 10), Juana lived with her husband and her two younger sons. All of her children were born in Mexico. The oldest son lived with his girlfriend and their 17-month-old baby. Although she said she regretted that her son did not finish school, she understood that he liked working better than studying. She said that her son wanted to take the GED test to get a high school diploma, but he could not do it; he did not even take the test. Juana said she did not speak English. Illiterate in her first language, she was taking Spanish classes in a church once a week. Although she went to school in Mexico, she reported she liked babysitting her teacher's baby, so she did not learn anything. Consequently, she wanted her sons to learn because she did not want them to suffer from being illiterate. Unemployed, she said she was very isolated, did not go anywhere, and did not know anybody.

Assumption and Rationale for a Phenomenological Research Study

Research Method: Why Phenomenology?

> At the heaven's doors, five travelers arrived one day. "Who are you?" asked the guardian of the sky. We are *Religion*—said the first; *Youth*...said the second; *Understanding*...said the third; *Intelligence*...said the following...and *Wisdom* said the last one. Identify yourselves ordered the guardian. And then...*Religion* knelt down and prayed; *Youth* laughed and sang; *Understanding* sat down and listened; *Intelligence*

analyzed and judged; And *Wisdom...* ? *Wisdom* told a story (Bucay, 1994).

The quote is a metaphor of my understanding of the meaning of phenomenology, a research method based on reports of the participant's experiences. During my years working with undocumented Mexican mothers, I wondered about the experiences these immigrants had living in a foreign country, with no documents, and struggling with their lives. Participants made meaning of their experiences during the interview in a process that described their journey. Unlike other qualitative methods that have the researcher as the main actor in the research process, phenomenology is based on the phenomenon, and participants are the ones who decide what is meaningful to them. The method has some common characteristics with psychotherapy in which the patient is the one who creates the session.

These two methods have in common the fact that the researcher, or the therapist in psychotherapy, functions as a facilitator, inviting the interviewees to talk about their experiences and the process is focused on the participant's experiences. Phenomenology offers a powerful tool to explore the participant's experiences using procedures that allow researchers to comprehend the core of the phenomenon. Polkinghorne (1989) states, "Experience is a reality that results from the openness of human awareness to the world, and it cannot be reduced to either the sphere of the mental or the sphere of the physical" (p.42).

Pollio, Henley, & Thompson (1997) said it best:

> What existential phenomenology offers to psychology is the possibility of overcoming the split between mind and body, spirit and world, and subjective and objective knowledge not by denying one in favor of the other but by demonstrating they are interrelated moments of a more dynamic and interconnected totality—that of contextualized human existence forever committed

to a world it can never totally comprehend but toward which it is continually directed. Only if such interconnectedness is acknowledged will it be possible for psychology to pursue its overriding aim: to describe human existence in a way that is methodologically rigorous and conceptually attuned to the complexity of this topic—the nature and meaning of ongoing human life (p. 365).

Interview Process—Procedures

The interviews started with the following question: *Tell me about your experience as a mother of a child in high school.* Probably relating to the words "high school" in the question, most of the mothers started talking about their experience with the school. Only one mother needed clarification about the first question. All of the other mothers made such comments as "It was hard because I do not speak English," or "I struggle because I do not speak English." The connection in their responses was school/communication/English. Subsequent follow-up questions were asked to clarify their answers. For example, if a participant said, "It was hard because I do not speak English," I responded, "Say more about that" inviting them to share more about their experiences.

Participants seemed intimidated during the interviews. They have known me for several years, but seemed unfamiliar with phenomenological research, and the recorder created a barrier between them and I during the interviews. Originally, I wanted to use an open-ended format, but given the nature of the participants, I realized it would not allow me to conduct the interviews successfully for the following reasons:

1. Since these mothers had little or no formal education, they did not know the meaning of some words. For example, when I asked, "How was your experience with that?" some of them answered, "Oh, I did not have any problem with that." Therefore, the word "experience"

seemed to mislead them. I was careful about the words I used; when they did not know a word, I rephrased the questions in simpler words, ensuring that the participant understood all the words included in the questions.

2. Silence made the participants uncomfortable. For example, if I did not have a question ready for them, they would make such comments as "Okay that is all I have to say" or "I do not have any experience; everything is just fine, just normal."

3. Since these mothers were very vulnerable, the order of the questions was very important. Even though I have known these mothers for several years, I realized that demographic questions created some tension in my interaction with them, therefore, when a participant did not talk about coming to the U.S., I waited until the middle or the end of the interview to address that issue.

Pollio, Graves, & Arfken (1997 state, when analyzing focus groups, that unlike a phenomenological interview "a group provides the text, and this difference affords possibilities and problems" (p. 260). Madriz (2000) notes that "focus groups allow access to participants who may find one-on-one, face-to-face interactions "scary" or "intimidating" [and offer] a safe environment where [they] can share ideas in the company of people from the same background." Pollio, Graves, & Arfken indicate,

> From her perspective as a Latina feminist researcher, Madriz feels that the voices of minority group members—those out of the cultural power structure— have not often been heard because of the unique nature of social science research. When participants are allowed to become part of a focus group, their voices combine and rise above a threshold that cannot be overlooked (p. 260).

After analyzing the participants' backgrounds, I decided to use a semi-structure interview format, and developed the following questions for the interviews:

1. Tell me about communication with the school.
2. Do you have a job?
3. How do you like your job?
4. How long have you been living in the U.S.?
5. How do you like living here?
6. What are your expectations for your kids?
7. Have you received any help?
8. Is there anything else you want to share?

Using semi-structured interviews made the participants feel more comfortable and the interviews flow more naturally. When a participant stopped talking or showed signs of uneasiness, I had questions in mind to ensure the participants would share relevant experiences that would allow me to gather meaningful information.

Setting

I asked the participants to pick a place, day, and time to meet with them. I respected the fact that, unlike earlier when I was helping them as a therapist, they were helping me and agreed to share their experiences with me. During the interviews, participants interacted naturally; sometimes the younger children were at home, the TV was on, or the husband was cooking supper. I did not ask them to change anything in their setting, even if, for example, the TV was loud and interfered with recording the interviews. I did not want to change their environment for two reasons; I wanted to observe them interacting as naturally as possible, and I wanted to show respect for their privacy. The principal investigator was trained in phenomenological research and conducted open-ended interviews. Participants were asked to sign an informed consent form prior to their participation in the interview. The informed consent was available in English and Spanish. A copy of the consent form is included in the appendix section of this book.

My Role as a Researcher

Being aware of my role as a researcher, I concentrated on putting aside my values, beliefs, or judgment. After having worked with these clients for several months, and in some cases for several years as a therapist, I made a conscientious effort to move from that role to become a researcher, observing them with an unbiased mind. As the research question indicates—"What are the experiences of these mothers living in the U.S.?"—the main goal of this book was to discuss the core of the experiences of these mothers living in the U.S. The most important part in the interview process and what makes phenomenology different, was the fact that participants decided what was meaningful to them. For example, when the first question was asked, "Tell me about your experiences as a mother of a high school student," all participants chose to talk about their difficulties communicating with the school. One of the most challenging parts of the interview was to remain in my role as a researcher. However, because they had known me as a therapist, I had to explain to them the interview's purpose. Some of them asked questions in the middle of the interview, as if I still were their therapist. For example, when one mother told me she wanted a divorce but did not know how, she asked me if I could help her with that issue. Another participant told me that her daughter did not finish high school and wanted to obtain some information about the GED. In such cases, I politely told them that after the interview I would be more than happy to assist them.

Additionally, because of my previous knowledge of the participants, they shared important information with me during my years working with them, I knew what to expect in the interviews. In some cases, participants talked about some of the problems they faced when they received treatment. However, their outlook was different at this time. Because I positioned myself in a different role, participants shared their experiences from a different role. As a result of that, the interaction changed, it was not a therapist-patient relationship this time, it was an interviewer-interviewee interaction in which the participant decided what was meaningful. My role was to listen to them, restate, summarize, or clarify, but I did not interpret or analyze their responses and that allowed me to interact from a completely different perspective.

Data Analysis

The interviews were audio taped by the researcher. All interviews were transcribed verbatim into written form by the researcher. Each participant was assigned an interview number and pseudonym. Participants' names and any other identifiable information were purged from the data. After analyzing the protocols with the Applied Educational Psychology research team under the supervision of Dr. Greenberg, we found, as illustrated in Figure #1 (page 59), the ground theme and emerging themes. The ground theme of this study is "Being an undocumented Mexican mother: Don Nadie." Other five themes emerged from the interviews: (1) Struggle (in four different areas), (2) Finances, (3) Language/communication, (4) Isolation, and (5) No control.

The interviews were conducted in Spanish and transcribed in English by the researcher. Spanish is my native language. If the research team experienced difficulties in understanding the transcribed text, I explained in different words the meaning of what had been said and together with the research team sought a more accurate word, expression or metaphor to capture the meaning of what the participant had said. Dr Velazquez, who is bilingual (English/Spanish) participated in the research process. Some metaphorical expressions that Mexican mothers used were translated word by word to communicate the original meaning of a metaphor. Some expressions from the Mexican culture were analyzed during the interview process. During my first years working with these mothers, some expressions were unfamiliar to me, but I was able to understand their meaning in the context of what was said. I became more familiar with these expressions after working with these mothers for three years. I was confident of my understanding of their spoken language at the time of the interviews and with the translations into English.

Methods of Verification

Dr. Howard Pollio's analytic procedure was utilized to interpret the data. His procedure involves the use of the interpretive group, the Applied Educational Psychology Phenomenological Research Team, under the direction of Dr Katherine Greenberg, consisting of graduate students of the University of Tennessee trained in phenomenological research. The members of the group read aloud verbatim all transcripts, thematized them, and found words and sentences in the transcripts that described the unique experience of each participant. The researcher continued the process of thematizing alone and returned to the group with nomothetic descriptions for the group to evaluate. The researcher continued to look across all the interviews so that "descriptive patterns and relations" characterized the entire set of interviews and identified comprehensive nomothetic descriptions of the interviewees' experience of the phenomenon.

Validity and reliability requirements were also embedded in the process. For internal validity, a bracketing interview with the group was done prior to conducting interviews. During this time, members of the research group were interviewed and each took turns describing their biases so that all members were aware of these biases during the sessions. External validity was addressed by sending results back to the interviewees, so that they could make comments, agreed, or disagreed with the findings. During the rigorous approach to research, no findings were included without the entire group's consent and without finding evidence in the text.

Table 1

Demographic Information of Participants

Participant's Pseudonym	Years in the U.S.	Marital Status	Employ Status	Number of Children born in the U.S.	Number of Children born in Mexico	Language
Maria	14	M	U	1	2	Spanish
Carmen	19	M	E	0	2	Spanish
Laura	9	S	U	5	0	Spanish
Guadalupe	5	M	E	3	0	Spanish
Barbara	20	M	E	1	2	Spanish
Rosa	14	W	U	3 (D)	3	Tarasco Spanish (L)
Leticia	10	M	S	1	2	Spanish
Mariana	9	M	E	2	1	Spanish
Teresa	22	S	U	0	6	Spanish
Juana	9	M	U	1	2	Spanish

D: Deceased S: Self-Employed
E: Employed S: Single
L: Limited U: Unemployed
M: Married W: Widow

CHAPTER FOUR

LISTENING TO UNDOCUMENTED MEXICAN MOTHERS

So when you are listening to somebody, completely, attentively, then you are listening not only to the words, but also to the feeling of what is being conveyed, to the whole of it, not part of it.
Jiddu Krishnamurti

This chapter includes an analysis of the research question along with themes emerging from the interview outcomes. The research question of this study is "What are the experiences of undocumented Mexican Mothers of high school students living in the U.S. who received social services?"

Themes

This section examines the ground theme of this study and the themes emerging from the interview analysis.

Ground Theme—Being an Undocumented Mexican Mother: Don Nadie (Mr. Nobody).

In phenomenology, the *ground theme* is a recurring and underlying theme that either in a latent or manifest form is present throughout the interviews. Unlike the *emerging themes*, which appear as the interviews progress, the ground theme has a constant presence. A tapestry is a good metaphor to illustrate these concepts, whereas the embroidery is more visible (emerging themes), the background (ground theme), either veiled or unveiled, sustains the embroidery. The ground theme of this book is "Being an Undocumented Mexican Mother: Don Nadie." Other themes emerged as the interview progressed.

The following quote provides an overview of the ground theme. Leticia described her expectations for her son, who dropped out of high school, and has no papeles (documents):

> He [son] does not have a social security, if we do not have any documents to be in this country...we are a Don Nadie [Mr. Nobody], right? And without a degree, it is even worse.

Her son did not have a high school diploma; but even if he did, he will not be able to go to college because of his immigration status. Participants did not explicitly discuss their immigration status, but the issue arose when referring to other topics such as job opportunities, expectations for their children, and family members they left behind in Mexico. Another example, Maria talked about the school experience of her son, who came to the U.S. when he was eight years old. He did not speak any English at that time. However, he knew that his classmates were making derogatory comments about him living in the U.S. and his Mexican heritage. Her son said to her,

> Oh Mommy, I do not understand what the children say about me, but they talk about me, they say that I am Mexican, and I should not be here. They said, 'You are Mexican, what are you doing here?' I think that it should not be that way because we are all the same, from one place or another place.

Many of these mothers' children were born in Mexico and came to the U. S. when they were young. Participants made some comments related to Being Mexican, Hispanic, or undocumented. However, their most revealing comments were subtle and understated. Mothers reported that they wanted their children to remember and be proud of their Mexican heritage. For example, when talking about her experiences in the U.S., Maria said,

Well, I, I have told them [her children], you seek a degree, that is fine, but even though we are here, we are Mexicans, and if we want to study, that is fine, but we always have to take into account the place we come from, where we are from.

Cultural values are one of the most important aspects in the study of immigrants. One of the biggest challenges Mexican immigrants face in the U.S. is the conflict that arises between keeping their own values and conforming to American values. Maria's narration of her experiences showed that she has constructed a new identity as a Mexican mother living in the U.S. but needed to preserve her traditions, values, and experiences from her place of origin. She told her son, "We are Mexicans," as a reminder of his origin and identity. However, when talking about school communication she reported that "Being Hispanic" was a disadvantage. Maria said,

Well, yes, he [my son] was just starting the school, no, I mean, like I speak something but I am Hispanic, and the other person speaks English, so we cannot communicate much, we have that auxiliary person [interpreter], to have the information of what happened, what he did, and at times, the school called us very often, the principal, but I do not know.

Another mother mentioned her immigration status in an indirect way. In discussing the family she left behind in Mexico, Laura mentioned hoping to get a "permit" to visit her mother in Mexico who she did not see in more than ten years:

I do not know, just learning English, learning English, what if one day, they say that after being in this country for a certain time, ones can put an application to, I do not know, to get a permit, I mean, I do not mean the residency, but a permit to be able to visit my mom in Mexico, we need that.

Yet, when describing her experiences living in the U.S., Laura said, *we are like a lion in a cage.* She knew she could not leave the U.S. to visit her mother because she did not have a permit (documents). If she did go to Mexico, she would have to cross the border, risking her life again. Guadalupe, whose husband was deported three times, said she did not know how to drive a car until she came to the U. S. She described her fear of the police in the following way,

> *Well, I was very scared, most of all, I was not scared at driving, I was scared every time I saw a police officer, I thought they were going to stop me, that was my biggest fear, but my husband taught me (driving lessons) a little bit, then my oldest son, he taught me very well, and then I started driving by myself, I learned to control the car, I would accelerate, and um, I had to overcome the fear I had to.*

Being undocumented is the root of the most excruciating problems that these mothers faced everyday such as unemployment, financial problems, lack of education, and isolation. Without "papeles" (documents), these immigrants are not legally allowed to work or live in the U.S. In their desperation to survive, they clandestinely work for companies that do not require documents. These jobs are poorly paid and abusive. Furthermore, undocumented immigrants cannot attain formal education to acquire necessary skills because of their lack of not only time and financial resources but also documents.

After analyzing the interviews, common patterns were identified. The ground theme is "Being an undocumented Mexican immigrant Mother: Don Nadie," which appears in all the interviews as the foundation of other themes (emerging themes). Participants mentioned their immigration status (undocumented) in either direct or subtle ways, using the words papeles (documents), identification, permit, residency, or social security cards, identifying this as an issue related to other difficulties such as limited job opportunities, financial hardships, fear of police, fear to be deported, and restrictions to leave the country to visit their family members in Mexico.

An important part of the ground theme is the mother's beliefs, values, and expectations. One of the questions in the interviews was "What are your expectations for your children?" Most of the participants said they wanted the "best" for their children but emphasized that they [the children] were the ones who decided what to do with their lives. Most of the participants stressed the importance of their children having an education; other responses included having a house, or a family, or just being happy. Here are some of the responses to illustrate this theme.

Maria, a married mother of three children said,

> We want them to take the buen camino [right road], most of all, as a mom, because there are always problems, so sometimes those problems come up before the age they mature, before or after, and one starts taking them, one wants to keep them young, we want them not to grow, no nothing, but they have to grow, be independent, well, that's it. My mom said, "Your children are borrowed." They grow up and become independent. One wants to keep them there, but it is not possible.

Carmen, a married woman and mother of two adolescents said,

> Um..., for them, um, I would like the best for them, but they are the ones who decide, they decide what they want to study, and you know, any parent wants the best for their kids, I would like for them to have a career, a good career, but they and the ones who decide, she, I do not know, she is not going to apply to college, I do not know what is going to happen with her.

Carmen seemed very uncertain about her daughter's plans for the future. She said she did not know what was going to happen, probably because her daughter struggled and was still struggling with depression. She emphasized that she (daughter) was the one to decide what to do.

Leticia, a married woman, and mother of three children, said,

> *Well, like any mom, I am a dreamer, I would like him to get married, to have his family, and at least to have a technical degree, a career, short but something to be able to defend himself, here, because, he does not have a social security, if we do not have any documents to be in this country we are a Don Nadie, right? [Mr. Nobody], and without a degree it is even worse, what helps him a lot is that he speaks English, and he is a very charismatic child, he has, he has a lot of, um, he is very good communicating with people, he has don de gentes [good manners].*

Leticia wanted her son to get a technical degree, even though she knew it is hard to attain formal education without documents. However, she also wanted him to get married, which seemed to be a strong value in the Hispanic culture. During the interview Leticia said, "Americans live together, they do not get married, but Hispanics do not do that." Interestingly, she, also, said, "If we do not have any documents we are 'Don Nadie' [Mr. Nobody]" and she wanted him [her son] "to be able to defend himself."

Teresa, a married mother of six children said,

> *Well, I would like the best for them, I advice them, I tell Diego, if you want to, if you wanted to, you could get a job and get a house, even if I have to pay for that, so he would not have to live with me, because you know that here in the U.S. kids get a house as soon as they are 18 years old. I tell him, I can, I, if I could and you wanted, if you bought a house, I would help you buy a house, so you can have your own house that is what I would like, you know he did not want to study, but this one, the one*

*who drives the car, he said he wants to study, and I tell
him it's whatever you decide to do, because if you want
to make them study they would not do it.*

Teresa already knew that her son was not interested in going
to school. He barely finished high school after taking the GED
test. Yet, she wanted him to have a job and was willing to
buy or help him buy a house. Another interesting part of her
response was what she said about Americans: "Here in the U.S.
kids get a house as soon as they are 18 years old." Like Laura,
Teresa believed that Americans do not get married; they live
together.

Themes Emerging from the Interview Analysis

The following themes emerged from the interview analysis (see
figure1 on page 59):

1. **Struggles/Barriers**
2. **Finances**
3. **Isolation**
4. **Language/Communication**
5. **No Control**

1. Struggle—*We struggled a lot*

The first theme was struggle, which was related to four other
different areas. When participants were asked, *Tell me about
your experience as a mother of a high school student*, some of
their responses included: *It has been hard; It has been difficult
because I do not speak English; I/We struggle a lot.* After being
asked subsequent questions to clarify their answers, participants
disclosed more information about their experiences with the
school and with other settings including doctors' offices, grocery
stores, and workplaces. Their areas of struggle included finances,
language/communication (including school communication),
isolation, and lack of control.

2. Finances—*Sometimes there is money...Sometimes there is no money*

All participants reported struggling with finances. Undocumented immigrants are not allowed to work in the U.S.; therefore, they often have no other choice but to accept underpaid jobs. Fifty percent of the participants were unemployed at the time of the interview. The book "Disposable Domestics" (Chang, 2008) offers revealing information about the financial struggle that undocumented women living in the U.S. face. In the chapter "Undocumented Latinas: The New Employable Mother," the author includes several studies on undocumented immigrant's wages. One of the surveys was conducted in 18 New York employment agencies and indicated that "illegal" workers earned as little as $175 a week and "legal" workers as much as $600. Another study, which was done in 1991, with Chinese, Filipina, and Latina undocumented women in the San Francisco Bay area, revealed that the majority (58 percent) of the employed undocumented Latinas surveyed held jobs in housecleaning and in-home care of children or the elderly, and factories. They reported their income was between $250 and $500 per month (2000).

Chomsky (2007) states,

> Immigrants do jobs that American citizens would not do—in Mexican president Vicente Fox's notorious words, "jobs that not even blacks want to do"—because they are not trying to live a decent life in the U.S. They could not, on their meager wages. Their frame of reference is their much poorer home country, and what seems like unlivable low wages here are worth a lot more there (p.17/16).

Compounding this problem, undocumented people do not qualify for any kind of financial help, such as food stamps, unemployment insurance, or health insurance because of their immigration status. Their children, if they are U.S. citizens, qualify for food stamps, health insurance, or other welfare benefits like the Women, Infants, and Children program (WIC). Another restriction was housing. These families lived in little towns in trailer parks or public housing apartments.

Undocumented immigrants have serious difficulties renting apartments or houses in the private market. Their financial situation and immigration status impede these immigrants to rent a private apartment or a house. Additionally, public housing renters must show proof of citizenship or residency, however, undocumented parents with U.S. citizens children qualify as public housing renters.

Here are some examples of these mothers' financial struggles. Maria stated,

> I mean, in a material way, sometimes there is money, sometimes there is no money, because when there is no money, one goes, and wants to buy more things than when there is money, and one says, 'What I am going to spend this money on?' or 'How I am going to manage this money?' When you do not have any money, you say, 'Oh, I want to buy this and I do not have any money' [laughing]. It is, most of all, like shoes, toys, clothing, whatever for them [children], or something for school, or if you do not have."

Guadalupe, a married mother with three children, whose husband was deported said,

> I thought about moving forward, even though I was by myself, I had to move forward, because if I did not move forward, if I gave up, nobody was going to say, 'I give you money for your rent, I give you money for medication, I give you money for this or that, nobody right?' So, I have to make myself strong, and work to move forward with my life, especially because, like I said, I did not have any help to get food or anything like that, so I do not have any help for the girl [daughter], I mean, just a little help to take her to the doctor.

Rosa, a single mother with three children, said,

> Well, my experience was very difficult because, when my
> husband had that accident [husband was murdered], he
> left me and my three girls, they were very young, the
> oldest one was six years of age, Maria; the other one,
> Lupe was 5 years of age; and Belen was 2 month of age.
> It was very difficult for me, I had to work, I had to find the
> way for my children, and I worked. I started working at
> 4:00pm until 11:30 at night, to be able to be with them at
> night, and um, in the morning, at 6:30 in the morning. I
> got up to, um, to send my girls to school, and to take care
> of my youngest girl, Belen, and until 3:30 in the evening I
> took care of them, and then I had to go to work, and um,
> it was a, it was a very difficult thing to me.

Barbara, a married mother of three children, when talking about
her finances said,

> One is very limited, one is, one cannot get the things one
> needs, because even the two of us work [husband and
> mother], um, with all the bills we have, you can imagine,
> we barely make it, and so if just one works, that would
> be impossible.

Juana, a married mother with three children, said,

> Ay [a Spanish expression used to show pain or hurt] I
> would like to work, I like working, um to help him, um,
> a little, but because we do not have enough money, you
> know that here, you have to pay for everything, you buy,
> you pay, I tell my kids today, I am going to cook a little
> egg to eat today because I do not have any meat, I tell
> them, we are going to cook a little egg for lunch today...
> it is all about paying bills.

Participants reported that they did not receive any help. One of
the questions in the interview was "Ha recibido alguna ayuda?"
(Have you received any help?). It is important to note that the

word *ayuda* [help] conditioned their response to something tangible like housing, food, or money. I clarified that help may come in different ways, such as counseling, interpreters, classes, or anything. After receiving clarification, participants still said they did not get much help. Also important to note is that most of these families lived in a *survival* mode, meaning they were so strained to provide their basic means to survive that other aspects of their lives were disregarded.

Furthermore, as I stated when analyzing the participants' lack of English skills and their resulting language barrier, most of these families had limited interaction with English speaking members of the community. As a result, they had limited, if any information, about their community resources, such as different social service organizations, schools, and churches. This lack of appropriate information, kept these families from participating in their children's educational process. Carmen, for instance, was very unhappy about her daughter's high school teachers and the fact that the school did not do much about her daughter to go to college. She also said that the school helped students send applications to different universities but that her daughter did not get any help because she had poor grades:

> No, she [daughter] did not tell me, she just said that they [school] sent student's applications to a college, and, um, they [school] recommended different kids, but they did not recommend her...they did not send her application, and that really upset her. She [daughter] said, what am I going to do if they do not recommend me? They did not send my application. They did not help her...she needs a recommendation letter to be able to go to college. I, honestly, do not know much about that, I just know what she told me, I even asked her if they had to send some paperwork, and she said yes, they sent recommendation letters for different students, they recommended different students. The ones who were admitted would send an application, so, she said she has to send an application after they send a letter of recommendation, but they did not recommend her.

On the other hand, Guadalupe talked about her daughter, who eventually received help for her health problems:

> Well, at the beginning, no, I mean, no, they did not help me much, just the school, they accepted her [daughter] in school, and then um, because I did not have any help I took her to a private doctor, and, um, then, um, I applied for health insurance and lately they gave me health insurance, and right now they are helping me, um most of all with medication, for her, when she is sick or in case of an emergency.

In contrast, Barbara sounded very upset and displeased when I asked her if she received any help:

> Just with the fact that they did not do anything when my daughter was raped, what can I expect, what else can we expect? We expect absolutely nothing...My girl, I mean, at her age, and they laughed at us, but God is very big, and people pay for what they do sooner or later.

3. Language/Communication—*English is Difficult*

One of the biggest struggles these mothers shared was their inability to speak in English. For example, Maria said,

> It is important, also, being here to learn English, it is the main thing, like when one goes to the school meetings, or go shopping, or meet with somebody, and says something, anything, you do not know what that is, you must know, at least, the basic stuff, but when you do not know it, one feels, like scared away or something, because you do not know what they are saying, and you do not know what to say, or if you want to buy something, and you do not know how to say it, how much it costs, or that, that happened to me when I first came here, he [husband] took me to the flea market, I

asked him how to say something, and he did not tell me, and he just said no.

When talking about her difficulties communicating in English Laura said,

Well, it is bad because, sometimes, somebody says something to you and you do not understand, you are like, 'I do not understand, I do not know what they are asking me, or they are expressing in a different way, because, I do not understand, I do not even speak English.' And that is bad, that I do not, that other people learned English and I have not, I am stuck, I do not know anything.

Most of these mothers reported that their children translated for them. Although sometimes doctors spoke in Spanish or the school had interpreters available, these mothers relied on their children to communicate. For example, when asked about the main struggle with living in the U.S., Carmen said,

I would think the problems with the language, because, like I said, in reality I have not done that, I have not gone to the school to file a complain, no, I know that because of them, I say I am going to go to the school, I will figure it how to do it, and they said, 'they [school] will not care...they do not care about the parents...they just believe whatever the teachers say.' They said they have already seen things and they do not care about the kids no matter how right a child is...They [children] just help me with things that I do not understand, but I am there hearing everything, they would help me with paperwork. Like my daughter was going to get her tooth pulled out, and um, I was there supervising what she said, the price, how much the dental insurance covers, stuff like that, but sometimes, I do not need any help, it is only when I have to say something, but I almost do not need anything because I have help in Spanish, the

doctor speaks Spanish and that [the doctor] is the most
important part.

Juana, who was illiterate and relied on her family to read her
bills, commented

> *Yes, when he [son] started working with him [an*
> *American friend] he started to, um, to speak and right*
> *now he, sometimes, um, if somebody calls and speaks in*
> *English, and because, he lives close to me, I would call*
> *him, and because his wife has a phone, so, I think, who*
> *knows what they said, so I ask them to come over to*
> *hear the message, and then, in the answering machine*
> *[laugh], who knows, I tell them, I cannot write my name*
> *in Spanish and you want me to understand that in*
> *English?*

When asked about their experiences with speaking English,
these mothers said they could not speak in English because it
was difficult. When asked if they had taken English classes, most
of them said they did not have time to attend. Working full time,
doing housework, and taking care of their children consumed all
their time.

Maria, when talking about talking English classes, reported,

> *Sometimes it is a lot of pressure, because we are*
> *different, because, one does not study English, one*
> *says, 'Yes I am going to do it,' but sometimes one does*
> *not do it, when one says,'I have problems speaking, for*
> *example, with the school, I cannot speak,' one says, 'Yes, I*
> *am going to do that' sometimes there is no time, so that*
> *does count a lot, having time, sometimes we cannot.*

Participants were aware that several organizations, especially
churches, offer free English classes to help immigrants learn
English. Unfortunately, most of these mothers said they felt
uncomfortable in an educational setting because they had either
very little or no formal education and, therefore, did not want to

write or read in front of other people. One of the places in which the language barrier became a real difficulty was the school. Mothers said they did not attend school activities and were unaware of the school rules.

School Communication:

Mothers reported that they did not communicate with the school. They stated that some schools had interpreters (English/ Spanish), but said they relied primarily on their children to communicate with the school staff. For example, Laura said,

> I ask her [daughter] things that I do not understand, I do not comprehend, and she would tell me, but sometimes it is difficult because, I would go to the school and they are all Americans and, one being Hispanic, feels like, like weird, right? And to ask something, it is complicated, but the good thing is that some people speak Spanish. There are interpreters sometimes and some teachers speak very good Spanish, and they would translate for me, they tell me what is going on with the girl [daughter].

Mothers also reported that they had not been to school many times. They said they went to school either at the beginning of the year for registration purposes or if "something happened." Leticia commented,

> No, I just went, in fact, in high school, I have only been there [school] like four times, two times to get him registered, and the other two times to talk when, when they told us about the problems he had, we went to talk with a bunch of people, and the last time when, um, to talk with several people to tell them we were going to take him out of school to start home school, so I have been to the school in four different occasions. The other times were for sports, I went to see him play, we were at the school, he played with his school team, but those were the only times I have contact with people at the school, and it was in English, they never had an interpreter for me.

Likewise, Teresa reported she did not go to school very often:

> Yes, I mean, I do not, one does not go to school. One does not go to talk with them or anything like that, and you know, sometimes they send a letter, saying we are going to have a meeting, but sometimes one does not have the time to go, because, sometimes. Like I told you, the job we have, and they do not have too many meetings, it is like, three times a year, I think based on the invitations they sent me, and yes, they would send a letter.

Mothers reported that schools did not have full-time interpreters and they [mothers] had to make appointments if they needed to communicate with the school. They also reported that some students offered translation services. Furthermore, they reported some undesirable situations. For example, Maria said that she has received phone calls from a school student saying that her daughter was sick and asking her mother to pick her up. Because this student spoke limited Spanish, Maria had a hard time trying to understand what he said. Mariana, on the other hand, said that she made several phone calls to the school, but when she started speaking in Spanish, the other person hung up.

Additionally, mothers stated that the school was not consistent communicating with parents. Mothers said they received letters from the school either in English or in Spanish. Because of this communication barrier, most of the mothers said they neither participated in any school activities nor understood the school rules. For example, Guadalupe, whose daughter was in special education classes, said that she did not know who decided to place her in those classes:

> I do not remember, I do not remember, but she was like, how can I put this? Like, they [school] were testing her, they [school] wanted to know if she was capable of doing the same things the other kids did, but they realized that

she could not do that, so they moved her to these special education classes.

4. Isolation—*We are like a lion in a cage.*

All participants reported having little or no interaction with English speaking people and with people in general. They said they stayed at home most of the time. With no documents to find a legal job, and the inability to speak the official language, they had little chance to have a fulfilling social life. They lived in small communities, but because of their lack of transportation, difficulties in speaking in English, and a limited social network, most of these participants showed little if any signs of integration. Instead, they showed signs of marginalization, having limited or no interaction with the mainstream community. Additionally, knowing that undocumented immigrants cannot leave and come back to the U.S. seems to create in them a sense of confinement and isolation.

Carmen, a married mother of two children, stated,

> *No, what happens is that, everybody speaks in English, at work, and I do not, and here I just have my family that speaks Spanish and [laughing] I just talk with my sister, she is like me, she only talks with the family.*

Laura, a married mother of five children, when talking about her daughter said,

> *But, sometimes, I mean, I know that she [daughter] is bored, she is here all day, she is bored. We are like a lion in a cage, we do not go anywhere, just go out and come back in, oh my God, that is bad. Where can we go? If one goes out needs money, if one does not have any money, what would you go out for? You are better off at home... Watching TV, getting bored. Yes and that is what bores her, sometimes she (daughter) goes out in the weekends,*

> *I give her [daughter] permission, she goes out with her*
> *friends, she asks me permission.*

Juana, a married mother of three children, when talking about her children said,

> *No, you see that I barely, I am at home all the time, and*
> *um, when he [husband] is off work, he would take me*
> *somewhere, and he would ask me, where are we? I do*
> *not know [laugh], I do not know—I tell him—because*
> *I barely go out, I am older than them [children] but I*
> *barely know people, I do not know anybody, and there*
> *are some people from Mexico, from my own town.*

In agreement with the literature review (Mendoza, 2002; Bressler, 1996), participants reported a strong sense of isolation. They said they did not have any friends and only communicated with their family members.

5. No Control—*Everybody was out of control*

Appearing several times in the mothers' narration of their experiences, the word *control* was related to three main areas, (a) The mothers' lack of control, (b) The children's' lack of control, and (c) The teachers' lack of control. The following examples illustrate this concept of lack of control.

Maria, a married mother of three, said,

> *Well, that was completely out of control, like I told*
> *you, well, no, in the school, we went in groups, people*
> *who spoke Spanish, he [son] went to school by*
> *himself, without knowing any English, well, it was very*
> *uncomfortable. Then he had problems in school, he had*
> *to go to an alternative school, because, he seemed to*
> *be out of control, he was obsessed with everything, and*
> *then, he was for a limited time there, it was very difficult*
> *because, I say, one explains things to them, the way they*

are, and they take that as if you were fussing or picking on them [regañando]. I am telling them that, things that are not, but one as a mom knows what is good for them, but one makes mistakes too, like they do, it is very complicated for them, because they want to think as adults, and we want to keep them like a little boy, do not go, do not do this, do not do that, they, at a certain age, they do not, I go here because I want to, buy me this because, we want them to take the right road, most of all, as a mom, because there are always problems, so sometimes those problems come up before the age they mature, before or after, and one starts taking them, one wants to keep them young. We want them not to grow, no nothing, but they have to grow up, be independent, well, that is it. My mom said, 'Your children are borrowed, they grow up and become independent.' One wants to keep them there, but it is not possible.

Carmen, a married mother of two, said,

[...] She [daughter] is in control now, but when she does not take her medication, she cannot control herself... She [daughter] has not taken her medication in two months, she did not tell me anything, and I noticed that she was acting different and asked her, 'Have you taken your medication?' And she said she did not have any more medication since more than a week ago, but she did not tell me anything...I started struggling with that, she would provoke us...she would say she is going to run away, oh yes, it is very difficult.

Laura, a single mother of five, when talking about her children said,

When they [children] go to school, sometimes one thinks a lot of things, and like why did she [daughter] change so much? Or when she is in a good mood, she would talk to me about her things, what she did, but when she is in a bad mood, she is like her older sister, a little less cranky, but, yes, sometimes one starts thinking, what did we do? What did we do to make her be like that or to have that attitude? I do not know, sometimes, she is just in a very bad mood. She comes home bored, maybe because she did not have a good day at school, but I thought a lot about that, I was like, this is very difficult, she goes to this school, it is like a different stage, more like, it is different from the other school [middle school]. In the other school, I would control her better, she was more affectionate, but in this school, everything changed.

Leticia, a married mother of three, thinks that teachers have no control over problematic Hispanic students:

[...] Teachers have no control, they cannot ask or demand more than they do, because we, Hispanics work a lot. Americans understand their language, a phone call from the teacher, or the principal, or anybody, with a dad, and that is just perfect. We do not, we must go with somebody else, like the counselor we have in the community, and, actually, he is overwhelmed with his job. I think he does not even bother himself to do anything, he would just send a little letter, and it was gone before I went to get it, because Pedro took it, signed it, and sent it back.

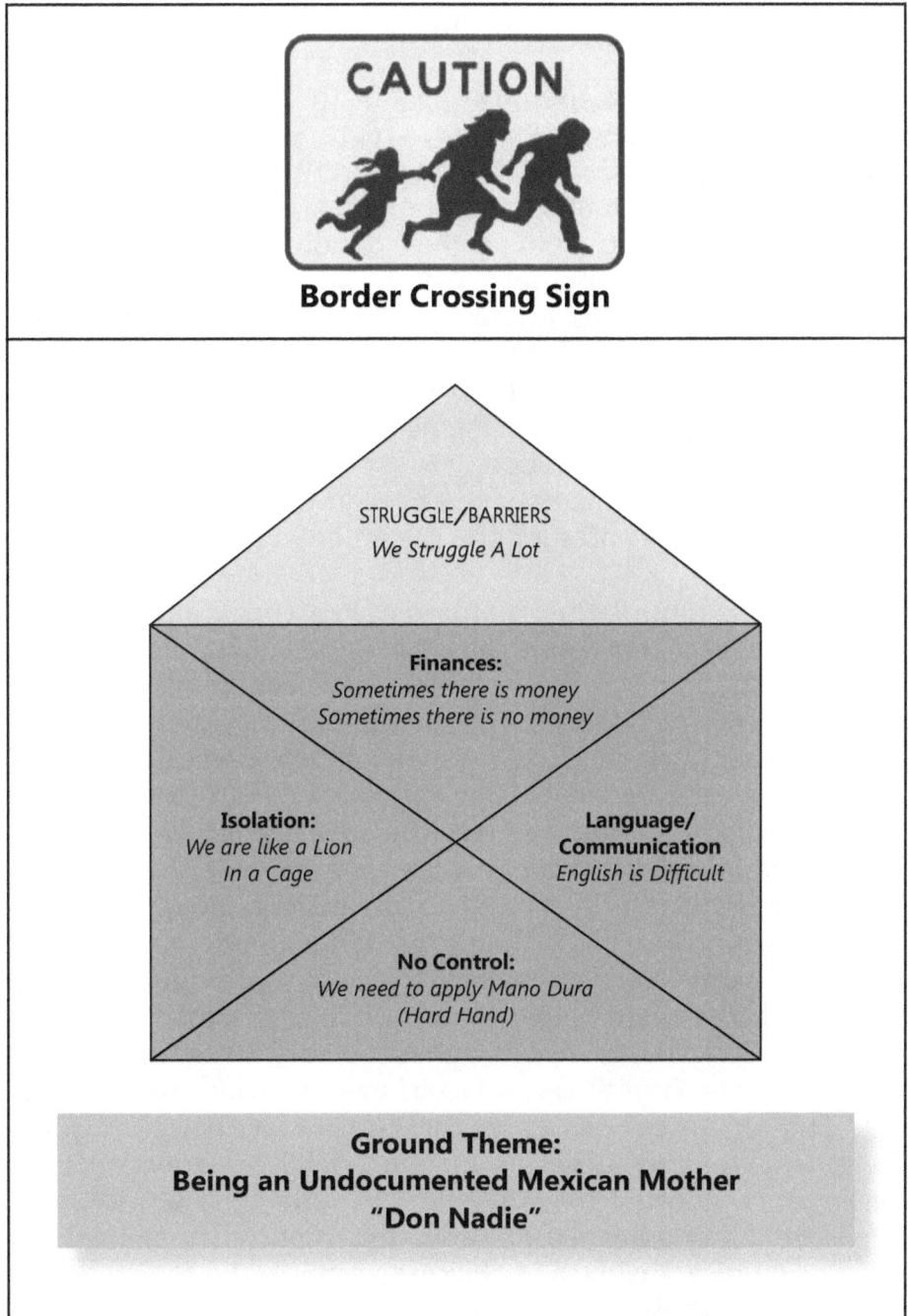

Figure #1:
Ground Theme and Emerging Themes from the Interview Analysis

Summary

This figure represents the outcomes of this research study. The caution sign or border crossing sign represents a family crossing the U.S.-Mexico border. As shown in the picture, the family is represented by the father who goes first; the mother is in the middle of the picture, holding their daughter's hand. This sign is present in several border roads to warn drivers to prevent car accidents. The ground theme, "Being an Undocumented Mexican Immigrant Mother: Don Nadie," represents the experiences of these mothers living in the U.S., and it is connected to five emerging themes, (1) Struggle, (2) Finances, (3) Language/communication, (4) Isolation, and (5) Lack of control. The ground theme is the background of the figure. It is present at all times and supports the emerging themes.

The first emerging theme is struggle. It is shown in the top of the picture and represents their struggle related to finances, language/communication, isolation, and lack of control. The second theme is finances. All participants reported that they struggled with finances. Fifty percent of participants were unemployed at the time of the interview. When asked if they received help, they reported that they did not receive any help. It could be inferred that their needs were so huge that the help they received was not enough to meet their requirements or expectations. The third theme is language/communication. All participants were monolingual (Spanish) except for one mother who spoke a native Mexican dialect (Tarasco) as a first language. Participants reported that they did not speak English. They said that "English was difficult" even the ones who did not take English classes. Some mothers said that they took some English classes but it was an uncomfortable experience. Other participants reported that they did not have time or money to afford English classes. Participants also reported that they did not communicate with their children's school. The fourth theme is isolation. Participants reported that they did not communicate with English speaking people. They reported that they only communicate with family members and coworkers in Spanish. The fifth and last theme was lack of control. Mothers reported a strong sense of lack of control for them, their children and their teachers. Despite their struggle and their lack of control, Mothers reported that they were hopeful about their lives, and had higher expectations for their children.

To summarize, participants reported their main struggles were related to their finances problems, inability to speak in English, lack of school communication, isolation, and a sense of lack of control. They stated that they had no control over their children, but they also reported that their children and teachers were out of control. Despite all these difficulties, they reported they remained hopeful, and had higher expectations for themselves and their children. They stated that they received no monetary help and only some limited help in the areas of counseling or social services.

CHAPTER FIVE

INVISIBLE WOMEN

*We humans are the only ones that create
borders for immigration, saying,
'You cannot go inside this line. This is the end of a
country, and here begins another one.' I am afraid our
time will be remembered as a sad period of human life
in which money was free, but people were not.*
Eduardo Galeano

This book aimed to shed light on the experiences of undocumented Mexican mothers of high school students living in the U.S. who received social services. The book provides a clear picture of these mothers' experiences. While the literature contains plenty of studies on Mexican immigrants, few research studies have been done on undocumented Mexican mothers and even fewer from a phenomenological perspective, a powerful tool to understand the *essence* of the human experience. Participants described their experiences through the interviews. They reported that they left their country hoping to find a better life. Forced to leave due to their socioeconomic situation, stripped from their family, homelands, and belongings, they experienced a strong sense of deprivation and loss. These women shared feelings of joy, sadness, hope, and a sense of striving to become part of the new culture. Despite their struggle to survive, the interviewees remained hopeful and expected their lives to improve.

When working with undocumented immigrants, professionals should consider the immigration experience as part of their journey and worldview. Our perception of the world is based on our experiences; therefore, immigrants' perceptions differ from nonimmigrants and have particular characteristics because of the impact of their losses, in some cases resulting in trauma. Kumar (2005), states that grieving is not limited to loss through death. For example, every time people lose a relationship or are faced with uncertainty, they grieve the loss of a predictable and safe world. Moving to a new place, losing a job, going through a divorce, being diagnosed with a life-changing illness, or separating from a loved one. Many changes in our relationship with their world are experienced as grief. Additionally, the grieving process varies from person to person depending on several factors, such as the person's psychological resources, social network, and resiliency.

Implications

Mothers' Voices:

The following paragraphs represent a hypothetical narrative drawn from quotes across the participants that serves as a summary of the themes/findings.

> I mean, in a material way, sometimes there is money, sometimes there is no money, because when there is no money, one goes, and wants to buy more things than when there is money, and one says, "What I am going to spend this money on?" or "How I am going to manage this money?" When you do not have any money, you say, "Oh, I want to buy this and I do not have any money" (laughing). It is most of all like shoes, toys, clothing, whatever for them (children) or something for school, or if you don not have. Well that is the way I see things...No, you see that I barely, I am at home all the time, and um, when he (husband) is off work, he would take me somewhere, and when he is driving he would ask me, "Where are we?" I do not know (laugh), I do not know—I tell him—because I barely go out, I am older than them (children) but I barely know people, I do not know anybody, and there

are some people from Mexico, from my own town that I
do not know.

They [her kids] just help me with things that I do not
understand, but I am there hearing everything, they
would help me with paperwork. Like when my daughter
was going to get her tooth pulled out, and um, I was
there supervising what she said, the price, how much the
dental insurance covers, stuff like that. But sometimes,
I do not need any help; it is only when I have to say
something, but I almost do not need anything because I
have help in Spanish, the doctor speaks Spanish and that
[the doctor] is the most important part.

The following sections include a discussion of the implication and recommendations for each theme and show their connection with other research on undocumented mothers.

Ground Theme—Being an Undocumented Mexican Mother: Don Nadie:

During the interviews, mothers said little if anything about their immigration status, instead treating it as an *unspoken* issue. Some participants mentioned the issue indirectly, when talking about not having a driver's license or not being able to go to Mexico to visit their family. Interestingly, however, most of the participants disclosed very private information when the interview was over and the tape recorder, which is very intimidating to them, was off. Several research studies, (Mendoza, 2002; Machado-Casas, 2002; Belliveau, 2007), when describing the lived experiences of undocumented immigrants, presented the theme of being undocumented, as an open and explicit issue, even when the topic was not brought by the researcher. Other studies, Villenas (2001), on the contrary, included the topic of being undocumented indirectly, as a tacit or unspoken issue. Willen (2007) analyzes the effect that "illegality" has on these immigrants. He states that it affects them not only in a legal way but also as embodied experiences. Their perception is affected by the way they perceive others see them. Their illegality determines their being-in-the-world. They may perceive this as there is "something wrong" with them as they are excluded from the system, and this perception affects their relationships with others.

As included in Chapter two, the negative perception of undocumented immigrants living in the U.S. and the immigrants' fear to be prosecuted as criminals represents one of the main problems when working with undocumented families. As for the negative perception, some participants reported that "being Hispanic was weird." The word weird may have a negative connotation; they did not say "different," "distinct," or "special." Therefore, it may be inferred from this statement that participants perceived that others see them as not only different but different in a bad way. The fear of being prosecuted was not mentioned during the interviews. Only one participant talked openly about her husband being deported. However, during the time working with these mothers, they said that they feared to be deported and requested information to obtain documents.

From my experience working with undocumented families, clients responded very well to the services provided. Their lack of trust appears as a natural consequence of the negative perception others have about Mexican immigrants, and their fear to be arrested or deported. Therapists working with undocumented families must realize that trust is an issue that needs to be addressed from the beginning of treatment. Building a relationship is crucial when working with undocumented families, and it includes showing empathy to the clients; responding to their demands in a professional way, that conveys firmness but also compassion; advocating for them; showing consistency during treatment, which includes attending all appointments, responding phone calls, and offering consistent advice. The key aspect to the relationship with these clients is consistency; that is, something that they lack in their lives, which have been financially, emotionally, and relationally unstable.

When contacting these mothers to be part of this book, they responded with enthusiasm. They were willing to participate and except for one participant, all of them agreed to meet with me, and seemed very excited to be part of this research. However, I think the reason they were willing to participate in this research was because they already knew me, and felt comfortable talking to me. Our previous connection made them feel comfortable participating in this study. During the interviews, participants shared their experiences openly and naturally, and the fact that they were undocumented was not presented as an issue or obstacle. They referred to that when talking about something else, which could be an indication of different things, either they knew that I knew that they were undocumented, or they did not feel comfortable enough to talk openly about it. However, this second option does not seem to be consistent with the fact that they brought it up even indirectly. For example, a participant said that she was not able to visit her mother in Mexico because of her lack of documents; another participant said that her son was not able to go to college because of being undocumented; therefore, they did not keep this issue secret, but it was present as the background from where they connected other problems.

During the interviews, participants did not talk about their emotions. Whenever they talked about emotions, was related to their children, for example they said that their children suffered in school for not knowing English and being unable to communicate with their classmates and teachers. They also reported that their children were discriminated by their classmates who made comments like "You are Mexican...what are you doing here? You should not be here...go back to your country." Another participant stated that her daughter did not receive help at school because "Some teachers are racist." Other participants, however, reported that they had positive experiences living in the U.S. and did not feel discriminated. Only one participant spoke openly about her emotions. She reported that she was extremely depressed and saddened with her life in the U.S. Her daughter was raped at the age of fifteen and her son was incarcerated for attempted robbery and possession of marijuana and paraphernalia in the street. She said that her children did not receive any help because of their Hispanic heritage.

Participants said that their experiences living in the U.S. as a mother of high school students were "hard," "difficult," and "they struggled a lot." It could be inferred that these difficulties they found in their lives in the U.S. included a high degree of stress, but they did not refer to their emotions in an explicit way. Several mothers said "I am forced to live here" (Yo estoy impuesta a vivir aqui). They seemed "resigned" to accept their hardships and remain in the U.S. Research indicates, Padilla & Ruiz (1973) that Hispanics are very private about their lives, and reluctant to discuss personal issues with therapists. During my years working with these mothers, they shared their emotions openly during our sessions, however during the interviews my role changed substantially. They did not see me as their therapist in my role as a researcher. It is important to notice that Hispanics tend to seek help within the family or social network when discussing their personal problems. When working with these mothers, they saw me as a therapist but also as a "friend" or a "helper," somebody they trusted enough to share their personal experiences. Because of their unawareness of the therapist-patient relationship, or being unfamiliar with the therapy setting, or their need to expand their social networks, some mothers invited me to go to the movies, or have lunch with them. Needless to say, I politely thanked them, but was unable to accept these invitations to preserve a strictly professional relationship.

According to Foulks (2004), Hispanic families are not likely to use community mental health services, resulting in significant unmet psychosocial needs. Historically, Hispanics have eschewed unwanted attention and the social stigma that often accompany mental health treatment. They prefer addressing problems within the boundaries of the family. Furman, Negi, Iwamoto, Rowan, Shukraft & Gragg (2009), state,

> The high potential for social isolation in transmigrants may be a factor that contributes to the development of high antecedents to distress. Transmigrants' lack of long-term residential bases, and their consistent

back and forth activities across borders and away from family, may inhibit their capacity to create positive social support networks that can ameliorate distress. This lack of social and emotional support may force transmigrants to rely solely on themselves to manage their stress. Subsequently, the culmination of stressors associated with constantly having to adapt to unfamiliar environments, work-related stress, and lack of social and emotional support may take a psychological and physical toll on many transmigrants (p. 168).

Cohen (2000) states that Hispanic use the term "controlarse" that means "being in control of oneself" to control their emotions. The author says,

Controlarse is a central concept upon which Latinos draw to govern the management of stress. It is a central mechanism for the regulation of behavior. It enables a Latino to exercise discipline over unpleasant events (disgustos) or troubles and upsetting situations (contrariedades). Controlarse helps to hold back outburst of feelings such as anger (corajes, enojos, o rabias) or the reactions of fear that result from such unexpected experiences as susto (magical fright). Control to one's emotions and mood leads to various states, such as resignarse (to resign oneself) no pensar (not to think; in this context to avoid thinking of a problem) or sobreponerse (to overcome oneself). Resignation reflects acceptance of a sorrow-full event and consent to fate, while no pensar refers to avoiding confrontation and the desire to suppress disturbing thoughts and feelings. Sobreponerse is the effort to overcome reactions to situations conductive to stress; It represent a Latino's willingness to confront a problem and a desire to alter his or her reaction to disturbance (p.205).

The next section includes the emerging themes and specific implications related to each as well as a discussion of how they relate to other research on undocumented mothers.

1. <u>They come to the U.S. seeking the American Dream and found a lot of struggle:</u>

During the interviews, participants reported their struggle living in a foreign country. Four main areas of struggle were identified: Finances, Language/communication (including school communication), Isolation, and Lack of control.

2. <u>Sometimes there is Money...Sometimes there is No Money</u>:

All participants reported having economic problems. During the first months working with these immigrant mothers, knowing the socioeconomic hardships they faced, I wondered why they remained in the U.S. However, in a relatively short period of time, these mothers disclosed information about their economic status in Mexico. Participants reported they were unemployed in Mexico, and if they had a job, their salary did not allow them to survive. Poverty in Latin America is different from poverty in the U.S (Galeano, 1997). Citizens of developing countries like Mexico do not receive social services such as food stamps or unemployment insurance, and if they receive government help, it is not sufficient to survive.

Participants reported they did not get much help since they moved to the U.S. but they mentioned the advantages of living here. Despite their struggle to survive, mothers reported that living in the U.S. is better than living in Mexico for several reasons including more job opportunities, better salaries, public school, and other advantages such as available education and free breakfast and lunch at school. The word "help" (*ayuda* in Spanish) is related either to money or other tangible financial assistance. When the question was restated indicating that help could come in different ways such as social services, counseling, or other forms of assistance, participants said they received some help. These findings seem to contradict research studies, Camarota (2001), that state that undocumented immigrants come to the U.S. to abuse social services. Mothers reported they received limited financial help. Because of their immigration status, participants did not qualify for food stamps, social security services, and other social service benefits. In some cases, if their children were born in the U.S. they qualified for limited services such as food stamps or the possibility of renting a public housing apartment, but they had limited help in accessing a doctor or therapist for themselves.

Mothers stated they did not have health insurance and their jobs did not include any benefits. Therefore, when they needed to see a doctor they had to pay out of their pockets. Chang (2008), states that undocumented immigrants are not eligible for welfare and many other public services. Additionally, their inability to communicate in English, lack of interpreters, and exclusion from the community, do not allow them to understand the purpose of social service organizations in the U.S. In other words, they did not know where to find help when needed.

Participants reported that despite their struggles living in the U.S., they made important progress. Research indicates (Valdivieso & Siobhan, 1992; Fix, Zimmerman & Passel, 2001) that undocumented families are the most vulnerable group, are poor by federal guideline, and face severe financial problems. Participants reported that their financial problems caused them isolation. They said they were excluded from the community, could not go anywhere because of their lack of money. Other factors contributed to this exclusion such as lack of communication with the school and the community in general, a small Hispanic population, lack of understanding of organizations in the U.S. The next section analyzes these mothers lack of integration in the U.S.

3. English is Difficult:

The language barrier emerged as the main obstacle in their process of integration into the new culture. Participants reported that they did not speak English. They stated several reasons, including lack of time and transportation as obstacles for acquiring English skills. Most of these mothers worked long hours or did housework. The urgency to survive seemed to get in the way derailing their plans to take English classes. They lived in a survival mode, and taking English classes seemed to be a luxury they simply could not afford. Participants, also, stated that they were uncomfortable in educational environments. Additionally, while several participants reported that their lack of English skills had limited their job opportunities, other mothers reported that they could understand "almost everything" they were told in English at their workplace and that their lack of English skills was not an issue in obtaining jobs. Several mothers said that "if they knew enough English to be able to communicate at work with other people, they did not need to learn more." All participants reported that listening was easier than speaking, an observation that matches Mexican women's role as listeners instead of talkers.

Unfortunately, socio-economic conditions, the necessity to survive in the U.S., the lack of time, and lack of education make acquiring a new language a complicated goal that most of the immigrants seldom accomplish. This difficulty exists despite that several organizations, including churches and social agencies, offer free English classes. In addition, some of these mothers are illiterate in their native language, making the acquisition of English even more unattainable. Chomsky (2007) states that immigrants attend ESL classes. Chomsky says, "The long waiting lists for ESL classes and the overwhelming trend for English to predominate among the second and third generation of immigrants from Latin America belie the common belief that immigrants are reluctant to learn English" (p. 110).

The implementation of ESL programs for undocumented adult immigrants seems to be crucial to integrate these immigrants into the mainstream culture. These programs must take into consideration immigrants' socio-educational backgrounds to be successful. The outcomes of this study indicate the participants have no English skills, which reduces their level of integration in the U.S.

3.1. I Have Been There [School] Twice:

One of the main goals of this book was to determine the level of communication between these mothers and the school, their understanding of school rules, and the degree of parental involvement. One of the most evident outcomes of this research was that the relationship between these undocumented mothers and the school was very limited. All participants reported that they hardly ever communicated with the school. The main obstacle in school communication is the mothers' lack of English skills along with the schools' lack of interpreters. Participants reported their unawareness of the school rules and a lack of interaction in the school community.

When working with immigrant mothers, educators must consider such factors as beliefs and values, cultural background, and level of education. Because many immigrants lack the education and English skills to understand the school and legal systems' rules (some of which are not explicit), their adjustment to a new culture is seriously limited. Another example of lack of communication and unawareness of the school rules is truancy. According to the Tennessee Department of Education, the school system requires 180 days of classroom instruction. Students' parents or guardians must be given written notice each time a student misses five unexcused school days. However, because of the immigrant parents' unawareness of the laws, lack of English skills and inability to communicate with school authorities, many immigrant children enter State custody because of truancy. According to the Mexican Department of Education, the school system includes mandatory classes from three to fifteen year old students, but truant children are not removed from their homes, and their parents do not go to jail; therefore, differences between the American and Mexican educational systems create confusion. McClellan & Chen (1997), among others, seem to be in agreement with this study. The findings of these articles indicate that undocumented Mexican mothers did not communicate or understand the school. As a result of this lack of communication clients reported feeling isolated.

4. We are Like a Lion in a Cage:

All participants reported feeling isolated from the community. Several factors contribute to this situation. Lack of documents seems to be the root of other problems, which creates a sense of non-involvement, reduces their job opportunities, and interferes with their interaction in the community. Cultural factors may exacerbate their limitations in social interaction. Many of these women experienced a cultural shock when coming to the U.S., and their lives changed in many different ways. These mothers also reported that their lack of financial resources impeded their ability to go places in order to have a social life. The following section includes these mothers' lack of control. When describing their relationship with their children, the school, and the school staff, mothers used the term "No control" consistently.

5. He was completely Out of Control:

Quinones-Mayo & Dempsey (2005) state, that one of the main struggles these mothers face is their inability to supervise their children. Mexican mothers complain that social workers empower children by advising them to express themselves, denigrating parental authority. Latina mothers express feelings of being betrayed by the professionals from whom they seek help. Immigrant children become the connection between their parents' values and American values. Teaching and advising parents about parenting skills or about developing alternative ways of discipline, requires understanding the parents' culture and children-rearing tradition. The findings related to control seemed consistent. Mothers agreed when describing their lack of control over their children. They pointed that they lost control over their children in their transition between middle school and high school. The expected conflicts that most adolescents face at this time in their lives become more difficult for teenagers from bicultural immigrant families, struggling between their parents' beliefs, values, and expectations, and the peer pressure they feel in school.

One of the areas in which they had no control was communication. During the interviews, participants reported that their children were the "interpreters" when interacting with English speaking people including the school staff. This situation gives their children power and control and made mothers depend on their children. The expected role of a mother, guiding and teaching their children, seemed to be reversed. Mothers' lack of control is also related to the dissonance they find when moving to the U.S. between the Mexican and U.S' values. During the interviews, mothers shared their beliefs and expectations. A specific question about their beliefs and expectations was included in the questionnaire. Findings show a consistent pattern throughout the participants. Unlike the stereotype, that portrays Mexican parents as a working class, uninterested in their children's education, all participants in this study strongly emphasized the value of education. Despite their lack of English skills, communication with the school, and unawareness of the school rules, mothers reported that they had high expectations for their children. They reported they wanted "the best" for their children. When describing "the best," participants focused on three main goals: (a) Having a family, (b) Having a degree, and (c) Having a house or a good job. However, all participants reported that the ultimate decision is up to their children.

Unfortunately, their desires clash with several obstacles impeding their children to be successful in school. Part of the literature review discussed in chapter two shows that Mexican immigrants value education but their urgency to survive and their limited formal education impedes them to help their children succeed in school. Participants reported awareness of their children's problems and struggles in the school. Saucedo-Ramos (2008) stresses the value Mexican families give to education and school and their preoccupation with their children's future. Parents guide their children about the value of education through *consejos* (*advice*), emphasizing that they do not want their children to face the same hardships they faced in not finishing school due to their socioeconomic circumstances. Instead, they want their children to break that cycle, thus having an opportunity for a good education.

Several researchers, including Quinones-Mayo & Dempsey (2005), emphasize that parents show differences in rearing children based on their parental belief systems. Mexican immigrant families living and raising adolescents in the U.S.

exhibit a particular belief system based on their previous educational background, life experiences, traditions, and values. Quinones-Mayo & Dempsey, state that the helping professions need to re-evaluate how they deliver services to the growing number of newcomers. The growth of immigration challenges the social work profession to first explore the complex matrix of diversity in a rapidly changing world of broken borders and then find new ways of delivering services to populations in need. Mexican mothers face a complicated task disciplining their high school children. Most of the conflicts are associated with this difficult stage of adolescence, such as consolidating identity, questioning parental values and house rules, as well as the dissonances between the Mexican and American cultures (Quiroga, 1996). While Mexican mothers try to preserve their traditions, adolescents imitate their peers as a way to be accepted in the new society.

Mothers reported different beliefs about themselves, their children and their lives in the U.S. Mothers revealed some interesting beliefs during the interviews. For example, most of these mothers reported that "getting married" was a value for them. Some mothers reported that, unlike Americans, who do not marry, Hispanic consider marriage a strong value. Other mothers reported that American children leave their parents when they are eighteen years old to go to college but Hispanics remain with their parents longer. Participants agreed when reporting that Hispanics have "strict values" while Americans are "more liberal."

Research studies, Mendoza (2002), show similar findings. In these studies, participants reported they perceived Americans as "cold and distant" and were concerned about an "excessive consumerism" in the U.S. It could be inferred that participants had a stereotyped idea about Americans that seems to prevail because of their lack of interaction with them.

One of the most revealing outcomes was their desire for their children to choose the "right road" [buen camino]. Mothers seemed to have a strong sense of sacrifice. They reported they taught their children the importance of being honest, hardworking, and reliable. During the interviews, mothers said that despite their inability to guide their children in school, helping them with their homework, or participating in their school activities, they do advise them to do well, and are involved in their children' lives by providing them a roof, food on the table, and a clean bed. In other words, some Hispanic Mothers cannot accompany their children in their educational process, but can be an important part of their children's lives by meeting other needs.

The next section includes recommendation for researchers, teachers, social workers, and therapists working with undocumented families.

Recommendations for Services

The following are recommendations for social service workers.

1. Implement effective approaches for educational social service programs that will help eradicate the pervasive and detrimental image of immigrants that portrays them as criminals or second-class citizens

2. Develop educational and social service programs that emphasize respect for the immigrants' culture and promote activities that include immigrants as a valuable part of the society

3. Create educational and social service programs that promote a welcoming, safe and inclusive environment in which immigrants can develop their potentials

4. Develop programs that emphasize the advantages that immigrant workers bring to the U.S., their contribution to the U.S. economy and cultural diversity

5. Strengthen or create links between these immigrants and the community resources ensuring these provide

interpreters and/or staff who have been trained in cultural diversity

6. Develop self-awareness and ensure clients are receiving services that meet their expectations. Develop surveys in Spanish to obtain feedback that allows social agencies improve their programs

7. Avoid judgmental approaches or culturally insensitive reactions that may damage the relationship with the client

8. Show empathy and sensitivity when working with these clients

9. Respect their cultural values and costumes

10. Learn about their culture and their parenting skill methods, which may be in disagreement with the parenting styles in the U.S. but need to be analyzed to better understand these clients

Conclusions

Based on the outcomes of this study, the following recommendations are offered to teachers, social workers, therapists, and health workers. Understanding immigrant culture is important for establishing a plan to integrate immigrants into the new country. While *acculturation* is the process by which a minority group adopts the values, customs, and traditions of the dominant culture, *integration*, by contrast, is the process by which a minority group adopts some values of the dominant culture but preserves its own culture. When working with undocumented mothers, social workers tend to impose their "way of doing things" on their clients, as if there were only one right way to respond to a situation (acculturation) disregarding the clients' culture and traditions. Coming to a new country includes some level of adaptation to the new rules, but showing respect for the client's background is crucial in establishing a relationship (integration). When working with undocumented families, educators and social workers should consider the suffering these immigrants experience and their specific needs resulting from socioeconomic situations, unique backgrounds, lack of English skills, and limited parental help for children doing their schoolwork.

Future research on the experiences of undocumented families is much needed. One of the most important aspects of immigration is the integration of immigrants into the new country. All participants reported lack of integration into the mainstream community. Findings indicated that the two main obstacles in the integration process were their lack of documents allowing them live and work in the U.S. and the language barrier. Despite efforts made by some non-profit organizations to help immigrants integrate into the community, their needs remain largely unfulfilled. The implementation of an immigration reform, however, is not sufficient to integrate immigrants. The idea of enacting an immigration reform that requires immigrants to learn English and American history seems insensitive and unworkable. Most of these workers cannot write or read in Spanish making those requirements unrealistic.

During the interviews, participants seemed reluctant to disclose information about their immigration status, which seems an indication of apprehension that can be an obstacle in the development of immigrant programs. Integration is a long process that includes several factors such as the development of a culture that respects immigrants and welcomes diversity. Findings in this study agree with the literature review: Mothers reported struggling with their finances, lack of English skills and communication, lack of interpreters, lack of integration in the mainstream community. They reported not getting help. One of the areas researchers should focus is the implementation of programs that help immigrant's families integrate into the mainstream community. Isolation is a huge problem and the consequence of policies that do not include immigrants. The following section describes the main areas for future research.

Areas for Future Research

Research should concentrate in the following areas:

1. Explore the impact that being undocumented has on the lives of these undocumented immigrant mothers

2. Explore how such factors as, lack of English skills and communication, financial strain, and isolation are interconnected

3. Compare undocumented and documented immigrant groups and explore how documented immigrants overcame the obstacles included in #2 (if they did) and what are the changed needed to overcome them

4. Explore empowering methods for undocumented mothers, that includes finding organizations and trained personnel in the community that can facilitate the information needed and help them develop the skills they lack to function in the new society

5. Explore the perceptions of these mothers that English is difficult to learn, even in cases when they did not take classes or seek help

6. Explore several beliefs of these mothers in depth. For example mothers reported that Americans do not get married; Americans children leave their parents' house by the age of eighteen, and other stereotyped ideas or myths about Americans

7. Explore the work conditions for these workers. Research included in this book includes undesirable situations and even abuse in the workplace. However, these mothers reported they felt respected by their supervisors and coworkers

8. Identify the reasons that made these mothers report not receiving help. Identify whether these reasons are related to their lack of understanding of the U.S. organizations (which is something several mothers reported) or lack of availably of services

9. Identify strategies to ensure more control with their children and with the school. Mothers reported not having control over their children. They also reported their children and their children's teachers were out of control. Explore this lack of control and its connection with other areas

Empowering Undocumented Immigrant Mothers

This book greatly changed my perspective of undocumented Mexican mothers. During my years working with these mothers, I was aware of their struggles, but the urgency of responding to their immediate needs distracted me from trying to understand their lived experiences overall. Each client's treatment plan had two or three goals to meet in a short period of time. The appointments were consumed with providing individual and family therapy sessions; teaching alcohol and drug education; checking their children's school grades and attendance; and teaching parent skills classes. During the research interviews, I was able to listen to them from a different perspective and became a better listener. Mothers were able to narrate their experiences as parts of a puzzle. Everything seemed to make much more sense. My outlook on their lives changed dramatically. I was able to see the whole picture and understand their experiences in a much deeper way. I was able to understand their being-in-the-world.

Beside my experience, I feel that educators should change their approach to communicating with undocumented parents. These Mexican Mothers show a desire to communicate with the school, understand the school system, and to be part of their children's education. Despite their enthusiasm, however, several factors interfere with their good intentions. Participants reported being financially stressed; some of them were unemployed or underpaid; all participants worked in the informal labor market. Their financial problems were structural rather than conjunctural; these mothers did not have the means to break the poverty cycle. Their lack of formal education, social contacts, and understanding of the labor market kept them from advancing in their jobs. Considering these factors, it is *essential* to ask how the community can best facilitate interaction with these mothers.

Their lack of integration transcends their inability to speak English. Other barriers seem more powerful than the language barrier. They reported in the interviews that even when interpreters were available in the school, they felt "weird" for being Hispanics. Their limitations communicating with the school, understanding the school rules, and lack of integration in the community, make them unable to understand their children's educational process. Their children were not successful in school, and the mothers seemed helpless or unable to assist them academically or behaviorally. All of these children were involved with DCS. Behavioral problems, truancy, substance abuse, domestic violence, and sexual abuse were some of the most common reasons for referral.

Children of immigrants experience specific difficulties such as identity issues, socioeconomic disadvantages, and family problems. Fortuny, Capps, Simms, & Chaudry (2009), state that children of immigrants deserve special attention because they face many universal risks to their well-being, such as lower parental education and family incomes, and are also adversely affected by factors unique to immigration such as lack of both parental citizenship and English proficiency. Hernandez (2004) agrees that undocumented immigrants have been neglected and that clear and efficient policies are needed to better serve undocumented immigrant families.

According to Pabon-Lopez & Lopez (2009), Hispanic students have the highest rate of high school dropouts, and they seem trapped at the intersection of two systems in crisis: public education and immigration law. The problems immigrants face have no quick fixes. Even in the best-case scenario, with a comprehensive immigration reform, undocumented immigrants need transition time to adjust to the new country: Learn English; understand the American culture; and most importantly, become part of the mainstream culture. Unfortunately, politicians' mixed messages about immigration have created confusion and uncertainty about the future of millions of immigrants who have come to this country to escape hunger and poverty. Understanding that the problem exceeds the school role in the community, educators must create ways to include these mothers in the school life, narrowing the gap between them and the school, and offering alternative ways of interaction besides having an interpreter in the school. Understanding their culture and listening to them will begin to empower these unheard mothers. The following recommendations are a good start to build a relationship with these mothers, an essential step in the process of integrating them to the new society.

Recommendations to Empower Undocumented Mothers:

1. Create literacy programs for those who have not received formal education

2. Create ESL programs that include specific classes for disadvantaged students, who have no prior formal education

3. Provide training to educators, social workers, and therapists on cultural diversity and specifically immigrant's cultures to better deliver services to these families

4. Focus on the advantages of immigration to help in the promulgation of a comprehensive immigration reform that includes immigrants as productive citizens

5. Promote social activities in the community and social networks that support these mothers through the

implementation of activities that include American and Hispanic families

6. Offer worship services, conferences, and different educational activities in which these mothers will have a chance to interact with other members of the society and channel their needs in appropriate environments. This can be extremely helpful for mothers who are victims of domestic abuse, or mothers with children with mental health and substance abuse problems. However, to develop efficient programs to empower these mothers, research is still needed in several areas.

From my perspective and background, as an immigrant myself, member of the Hispanic heritage, and social service therapist, I am including my personal reflections about this study.

Personal Reflections

One of the greatest rewards I experienced when working with undocumented mothers, was their profound gratitude, demonstrated in various ways. Inviting me to eat a special dish from Mexico, to their children's baptism or birthday celebration; giving me a picture of the virgin of Guadalupe; and making such comments as "I do not know what I am going to do when you close my case." Their gratitude, made me feel loved and respected. During the interviews, these mothers were extremely attentive, cooperative, and excited to be part of this research. An interesting part of the interview process was observing the participants' nonverbal behavior, body language, gestures, and facial expressions. Only one mother showed signs of frustration and anger as she reported being extremely depressed with her family's circumstances involving a pregnant teenage daughter and a son in prison. The rest of the participants were very pleasant and attentive. Even when narrating difficult situations, they maintained a positive attitude and remained hopeful about their lives and families. They also exhibited a sense of acceptance, progress, and patience.

For these families, I discovered some invisible borders, not physical or territorial, that are hard to trespass. Stronger than the physical ones, these borders are lack of integration, financial hardships, discrimination, and isolation. I truly hope that politicians approve an immigration reform that helps integrate these immigrants, and respect them in any way possible. The United States is a country of immigrants, a land of opportunities. The U.S. Constitution starts with the following statement: "We The People." It does not say "We Americans" or "We, legal or illegal immigrants." It says "We the People." Undocumented immigrants are counted by dozens of millions; but they are individually mothers, sisters, and daughters, fathers, brothers, and sons. They have dreams and hopes. They are the *Mojados* who were excluded from their own country. They want to succeed in a country that has the capability to offer them what was denied in their own homelands: freedom, opportunity and prosperity.

REFERENCES

Adler, L (1978). *Up in smoke*. Paramount Pictures. U.S.

Arjona, R. (2000). El *Mojado*. Album *Adentro*. http://www.youtube.com/watch?v=61y0ASGxtEA

Bacon, D. (2008). *Illegal People. How globalization creates migration and criminalizes immigrants*. Beacon Press, Boston.

Balderrama, M. V. & Diaz-Rico, L. T. (2006) *Teaching performance expectation for educating English learners*. Pearson Education, Inc.

Barnes, R. F. (1969). *Conflicts of cultural transition: A review of dilemmas faced by the Mexican farm worker and his family*. California University, Davis. Department of Applied Behavioral Sciences.

Belliveau, Michele (2007). *Navigating the policy context: Experiences of undocumented Mexican mothers in a new suburban immigrant community. A dissertation in social welfare*. University of Pennsylvania. ProQuest Information and Learning Company.

Berger, P. L. & Luckmann, T. (1966). *The social construction of reality: A treatise in the sociology of knowledge. Garden City, NY: Doubleday*.

Bonnefil, M. C. & Jacobson, G. F. (1979). *Family crisis intervention*. Clinical Social Work Journal. 7(3), 200-213. Human Sciences Press.

Borjas, G. J. (2001). *Heaven's Door: Immigration policy and the American economy.* Princeton University Press.

Bressler, S. L. (1996). *Voices of Latina migrant mothers in rural Pennsylvania.* In Flores, J. L. Children of La Frontera: Binational Effort to serve Mexican migrant and immigrant students (311-324).

Bucay, J. (1994). *Recuentos para Demian: Los cuentos que contaba mi analista.* Ed. Del Nuevo Extremo. Buenos Aires. Argentina. [Tales for Demian: The tales that my therapist told. Ed Del Nuevo Extremo. Buenos Aires. Argentina].

Bullough, R. (2002). *Thoughts on teacher education in the USA.* Journal of Education for Teaching 28(3) pp.233-237.

Camarota, S. A. (2001). *Immigration from Mexico: Assessing the impact on the United States.* Center for Immigration Studies. 64 pp.

Camarota, S. A. (2012). *Immigration in the United States: A Profile of America's Foreign-Born Population.* Center for Immigration Studies. p. 9.

Census 2010. (2010). http://www.census.gov

Chang, G. (2008). *Disposable Domestics. Immigrant women workers in the global economy.* South End Press. Cambridge, Massachusetts.

Chomsky, A. (2007). *They take our job and 20 other myths about immigration.* Beacon Press. Boston.

Cohen, L. M. (1985). *Controlarse and the problems of life among Latino immigrants.* In Vega, W. A. *Stress & Hispanic mental health: Relating research to service delivery.* National Institute of Mental Health (DHHS), Rockville, Md. Superintendent of Documents, U. S. Government Printing Office, Washington, DC.

Driessen, G., Frederik, S., Sleegers, P. (2005). *Parental involvement and educational achievement*. British Educational Research Journal, 31(4), pp.509-532.

Dudley-Marling, C. (2004) *The social construction of learning disabilities*. Journal of Learning Disabilities, 37(6) pp. 482-489.

Fiske, S.T. (1993). *Controlling other people. The impact of power on stereotyping*. American Psychological Association, 48(6), pp.621-628.

Fix, M., Zimmerman, W. & Passel, J. S. (2001) *The Integration of immigrant families in the U.S.* The Urban Institute. Washington D.C. 66pp.

Flannery, R. B. & Everly, G. S. (2000). *Crisis Intervention: A review*. International Journal of Emergency Mental Health, 2(2), pp.119-125

Fortuny, K., Capps, R., Simms, M. & Chaudry, A. (2009). *Children of immigrants: National and State characteristics*. The Urban Institute. Washington D.C. 18pp.

Foulks, E. F. (2004). *Cultural variables in psychiatry*. Psychiatric Times, 21, 28-29.

Freire, P. (1970). *Pedagogy of the oppressed*. New York: Herder & Herder.

Fukuyama, F. (2006). *Identity, immigration, and democracy*. Journal of Democracy, 17(2).

Furman, R., Negi, N. J., Iwamoto, D. K., Rowan, D. Shukraft, A. & Gragg, J. (2009). *Social Work Practice with Latinos: Key Issues for Social Workers*. National Association of Social Workers.

Galeano, E. (1997). *Open veins of Latin America: Five centuries of the pillage of a continent*. Monthly Review Press.

Garret, J. E. & Holcomb, S. (2005) *Meeting the needs of immigrant students with limited English ability.* Journal of International Education, 35, p.49-62.

Gergen, K. J. (1985). *The social constructionist movement in modern psychology.* American Psychologist, 40(3), 266-275.

Gil, R. M. & Vazquez, C. I. (2002). *The Maria paradox (La paradoja de Maria).* Thorndike Press. Waterville, Maine.

Glazer, N. (1995). *Immigration and the American future.* Manhattan Institute and the Pacific Research Institute.

Greenberg, K. (2000). *Cognitive enrichment advantage. Family-School partnership handbook.* Skylight Professional Development.

Greenfield, P. M., Trumbull, E., Keller, H., Rothstein-Fisch, C., Suzuki, L.K., & Quiroz, B. (2006) *Cultural conceptions of learning and development. In* Alexander, P. A. & Winne, P. H. Lawrence. Handbook of Educational Psychology. Erlbaum Associates, Publishers. Mahwah, New Jersey. London. 29(675-692).

Gunderson, L. *(2000). Voices of the teenage diasporas.* Journal of Adolescent & Adult Literacy, v43 n8 p692-706

Hancock, T. U. (2007). *Sin papeles: Undocumented Mexicanas in the rural United States.* Journal of Women and Social Work. 22(2) Pp.175-184

Hanley, J. (1999). *Beyond the tip of the iceberg: Five stages toward cultural competence.* Reaching Today's Youth. 3(2) pp. 9-12

Henderson, A. & Mapp, K. (2002). *A new wave of evidence: the impact of school, family, and community connections on student achievement. Annual synthesis 2002.* (Austin, TX, Southwest Educational Development Laboratory). Pp.1-241.

Hernandez, D. J., (2004), *Demographic change and the life circumstances of immigrant families.* The Future of Children, Special Issue on Children of Immigrants, 14(2):16-47.

Hoefer, M., Rytina, N. & Baker, B. C. (2009). *Estimates of the unauthorized immigrant population residing in the United States: January 2009.* Office of Immigration Statistics, Policy Directorate, U.S. Department of Homeland Security. http://www.dhs.gov/xlibrary/assets/statistics/publications/ois_ill_pe_2009.pdf

Hondagneu-Sotelo, P. (1996). *Unpacking 187: Targeting mejicanas. Immigration and ethnic communities: A focus on Latinos.*

Horton, S. (2008). *A Mother's heart is weighed down with stones: A phenomenological approach to the experience of transnational motherhood.* Cult Med Psychiatry 33:21-40. Immigration and Nationality Act (1952).

Immigration Reform and Control Act of 1986 (IRCA). http://www.oig.lsc.gov/legis/irca86.htm

Johnson, A. G. (1997). *The gender knot: Unraveling our patriarchal legacy.* Temple University Press. Philadelphia.

Krishnamurti, J. Quotes. http://www.jiddu-krishnamurti.net

Kumar, S. M. (2005). *Grieving mindfully. A compassionate and spiritual guide to coping with loss.* New Harbinger Publications, Inc.

Lazarus, Emma. *Words at the base of the statue of liberty.*

Lenz, L. (2002). *Been there, done that, Mr. President.* Journal of Staff Development. 23(4), 84.

Lewis, Anne (2007). Morristown: In the air and the sun. U.S.

Machado-Casas, M. (2002). *The Politics of organic phylogeny: The art of parenting and surviving at transnational multilingual Latino indigenous immigrants in the U.S.* The University of North Carolina Press.

Madriz, E. (2000). *Focus groups in feminist research.* In Denzin, N. & Lincoln Y. (Eds.), *Handbook of qualitative research* (2nd ed., pp. 835-850). Thousand Oaks, CA: Sage.

McClelland, J., & Chen, C. (1997). *Standing up for a son at school: experiences of a Mexican immigrant mother.* Hispanic Journal of Behavioral Sciences.

McIntosh, P. (1988). *White privilege and male privilege: A personal account of coming to see correspondences through work in women's studies.* Working Paper No. 189. 25 pp.

Mendoza, M. (2002). *Latino immigrant women in Memphis.* Center for Research on women. The University of Memphis.

Merleau-Ponty, M. (2002). *Phenomenology of perception.* Routledge Classics. London and New York.

Miller, P. C. & Endo, H, (2004). *Understanding and meeting the needs of ESL students.* Phi Delta Kappa, 8, 786-791.

Mortensen R.W. (2009). *Illegal, but not undocumented. Identity theft, document fraud, and illegal employment.* Center for Immigration Studies (CIS).

National Council of La Raza (2003). *NCLR Agenda for Hispanic families: A public policy briefing book.* National Council of La Raza, Washington, DC.

Nieto, S. (2002). *Language, culture, and teaching: Critical perspectives for a new century.* Mahwah, NJ: Erlbaum.

The No Child Left Behind Act (2001). http://www2.ed.gov/nclb/landing.jhtml

Okagaki, L. & Sternberg, R. K. (1993). *Parental beliefs and children's school performance.* The Society for Research in Child Development, Inc.

Pabon-Lopez, M. & Lopez, G. (2009) *Persistent inequality: Contemporary realities in the education of undocumented Latina/o students.* Critical Educator. Routledge.

Padilla, A., Ruiz, R. (1973). *Latino mental health: A review of literature.* National Institute of Mental Health (DHEW). Rockville, Md. 195p.

Passel, J. S. & Fix, M. (2001) *U.S. Immigration at the beginning of the 21st Century.*

Testimony before the subcommittee on immigration and claims hearing on "The U.S. population and immigration" Committee on the Judiciary, U.S. House of Representatives. Immigration Studies Program. The Urban Institute.

Passel, J. S. & Cohn, D. (2008). *Trends in unauthorized immigration: Undocumented inflow now trails legal inflow. Washington, DC: Pew Hispanic Center.*

Payne, M. (2005) *The origins of social work: Change and continuity.* Basingstoke: Palgrave Macmillan.

Paz, O. (1950). *The labyrinth of solitude, The other Mexico, Return to the labyrinth of solitude, Mexico and the United States, The philanthropic ogre.* New York, Grove Press.

Polkinghorne, D. E. (1989). *Phenomenological research methods.* In Valle, R. S. & Steen Halling (Eds), Existential phenomenological perspectives in psychology (pp.41-60). New York, NY: Plenum Press.

Pollio, H. R, Graves, T. R., & Arfken, M. (1997). *Qualitative methods.* In Leong, F. T. L. & Austin, J. T. The psychology research handbook: a guide for graduate students and research assistants. Sage Publications Inc. (pp.254-276). Pollio, H. R., Henley, T. B., & Thompson, C. J. (1997). *The phenomenology of everyday life.* New York, NY: Cambridge University Pres.

Portes, A. (2006). *The new Latin nation: Immigration and the Hispanic population of the United States.* Monográfico sobre globalización e inmigración (16) p.55

Quinones-Mayo, Y. & Dempsey, P. (2005). *Finding the bicultural balance: Immigrant Latino mothers raising "American" adolescents.* Child Welfare League of America. LXXXIV(5), (pp.649-667).

Quiroga, Susana (1997). *Adolescencia: Del goce organico al hallazgo de objeto* (Spanish edition). Eudeba. Facultad de Psicologia, Oficina de Publicaciones, Ciclo Basico Comun, Universidad de Buenos Aires.

Ramirez, A. (2003) *Dismay and disappointment: Parental involvement of Latino immigrant parents.* Urban Review, 35(2) p93-110.

Riger, S. (1992). *Epistemological debates, feminist voices: Science, social values, and the study of women.* University of Illinois at Chicago. American Psychological Association, 47(6),730-740

Roessingh, H. (2006). *The Teacher is the key: Building trust in ESL high school programs.* The Canadian modem language review/La Revue canadienne des langues vivantes,62(4).

Sandler, J., Dreher, A., Dare, C., Holder, A. (1973). *The patient and the analyst; the basis of the psychoanalytic process.* New York, International Universities Press.

Sartor, C. E. & Youniss, J. (2002). *The relationship between positive parental involvement and identity achievement during adolescence.* Journal of Adolescence, 37(146).

Saucedo-Ramos, C. (2008). *Estudia para que no te pase lo que a mí: Narrativas culturales sobre el valor de la escuela en familias mexicanas. [Study so you do not have to go through the things I went through: Cultural narratives on the value of school in Mexican families.* Journal of Latinos and Education 2(4), 197-216. Lawrence Erlbaum Associates, Inc.

Sconyers, N. (1996). *What parents want: A report on parents' opinions about public schools.* Center on Families Communities. Schools and Children's Learning.

Seivers, L., McCargar, J. (2005) *A handbook for principals. NCLB.* Tennessee Department of Education.

Urrieta, K. Quach, L. H. (2000). *My language speaks of me: Transmutational identities inL2 acquisition.* The High School Journal Vol.8 (1).

Valdivieso, R., Siobhan, N. (1992). *Look me in the eye: A Hispanic cultural perspective on school reform.* Paper commissioned for at-risk evaluation. Information analysis.

Valencia, R., Valenzuela, A, Sloan, K. & Foley, D. E. (2001). *Let's treat the cause, not the symptoms: equity and accountability in Texas revisited.* Phi Delta Kappan. 83(4), 318-326.

Valencia, R. & Black, M. (2002). Mexican *Americans don't value education! The basis of the myth, mythmaking, and debunking.* Journal of Latinos and Education, 1(2), pp.81-103.

Valle, R. S., Halling, S. (1989). *Existential-phenomenological perspectives in psychology: exploring the breadth of human experience: with a special section on transpersonal psychology.* New York: Plenum Press.

Villenas, S. (2001). *Latina Mothers and small-town racisms: Creating narratives of dignity and moral education in North Carolina.* Anthropology & Education Quarterly 32(1)3-28.

Wells, H. (1968). *The modernization of Puerto Rico: A political study of changing values and institutions.* Cambridge, MA: Harvard University Press.

Willen, S. (2007). *Toward a critical phenomenology of 'illegality:' State power, criminalization, and Abjectivity among undocumented migrant workers in Tel Aviv, Israel.* International Migration 45(3): 8-36.

APPENDIX

INTERVIEW
Participante #7 (Spanish)

Madre mexicana indocumentada casada con tres niños (edades 19, 6, y 3 años).

Monolingüe (solo habla español). Emigraron a los EUA en el año 1999. Padres trabajan en su propio negocio. Los padres y el hijo mayor son indocumentados; los dos hijos pequeños nacieron en los EE.UU. El hijo mayor no termino el colegio secundario (high school). Madre describe problemas para comunicarse con la escuela y la comunidad en general.

Entrevistador: Me gustaría que me cuentes como ha sido tu experiencia como mamá mexicana de un chico de high school...

Participante: Me involucré mucho en sus problemas porque, de hecho, Diego empezó estudiando perfectamente bien, le exigíamos demasiado, en cuanto él entro al high school nuestro negocio nos empezó a absorber muchísimo, entonces, entonces, dejamos de lado la responsabilidad que teníamos de exigirle a Diego, calificaciones y grados y que estudiara, entonces, conforme fue avanzando nuestro negocio, a lo mejor hubo manera de que (pausa). Se le dio un vehiculo a Diego para que se fuera a la escuela, ya no se iba en el bus, y de ahí empezaron nuestros grandes problemas, porque también se le dio celular para comunicarnos, ya lo veíamos menos tiempo. El otro pequeñín siempre andaba con nosotros, entonces, bueno, fue *catastrófico*, el comienzo de nuestro negocio porque al haber dinero, había para más cosas y nos descuidamos de su escuela, el otro pequeñito no iba a la escuela, Diego si iba, entonces él empezó a andar manejando, traía dinero, traía celular, y ya traía a sus amigos en el vehiculo y se salía mucho de clases. Cuando entraba a clase era un niño bien portado, todos lo estimaban, veían que cumplía bien y todo, pero cuando a él se le ponía de que "hoy no voy a la escuela, hoy me voy de *pinta*", se iba con sus cuates, y los invitaba, "Ey, traigo dinero, vámonos a pasear, los llevo a tal ciudad, lo llego a la otra ciudad, los llevo para acá..." (El nombre de las ciudades no se incluye por cuestiones de confidencialidad). Y se iba la bola, cinco o seis amiguitos y se iban con él a pasear...

E: Aja...

P: Entonces, de esto no me lo fueron comunicando a mí por parte de la escuela, o me lo hacían, a él le decían que me lo comunicara y él no me daba ningún papel, nunca, yo a veces ni me enteraba, yo no sabía nada de esto, hasta que pasó cerca de año y medio con toda esta problemática, yo ni enterada estaba...

E: Aja ¿Ni enterada... ?

P: No, y yo, conciente de que mi hijo iba bien. "¿Cómo vas Diego?"; "No, voy bien, voy bajo una materia pero le voy a echar las ganas y voy bien". Y todos creyéndole, el papá y la mamá...

E: Claro...

P: Pero fue tremendo cuando, la decepción, cuando, bueno, casi fueron dos años, cuando yo me enteré...

E: ¿Cómo fue que te enteraste?

P: Me enteré por unas amigas, no por la escuela, porque yo creo que Diego falsificaba mi firma, y le decían que la mamá se presentara, que él llevaba amigas, amigas mías y las llevaba y decían que eran sus tías, y firmaban por mí, bueno...

E: ¿Y ellas te contaron?

P: No, Diego me contó, luego, "No, es que un día una amiga fue, una amiga tuya fue por su hija". Le dije, "Mire, mi mamá está trabajando, ya ve que está embarazada, y anda con problemas con el bebé, entonces no sé si usted quisiera firmar, nada más de que, le van a decir unas cosas mías ahí, me van a regañar y voy a estar allí". Ella le respondió, "Ah, no, si, Diego, como no, ahí me saludas a tu mamá". La señora fue y firmó, y creo que anteriormente Diego me firmaba todos los documentos que a mí me enviaban, él, él firmaba, y cuando quería sus permisos iba de pinta, él firmaba, una responsiva mía que yo solicitaba que el niño no fuera a clase...

E: ¿Y la escuela nunca dijo nada... ?

P: La escuela bien, perfecto, yo siento que para los hispanos la escuela no pone *mano dura* en cuanto a los problemas que están, porque el niño hispano es problemático en si, el niño hispano es problemático, entonces le dicen "Cállate...siéntate", y ellos contestan en español y no quieren a veces poner atención o hacer caso de lo que les dicen. Yo siento, que se sienten bien felices, cuando los pasan a sus clases de hispanos, ELL (Alumnos que aprenden inglés como segundo idioma por las siglas en inglés), y allí se la pasan súper, puro relajo (pausa).

E: ¿Los niños o los profesores?

P: No, los compañeros, los niños. Los maestros, *yo siento que se les salen de la mano*, ellos no pueden exigir más, porque *nosotros los hispanos trabajamos mucho*, y el americano se entiende en su idioma, una llamadita del profesor, o del director, o de alguien con algún papá y perfecto, y a nosotros no, tendrían que ir con otra persona que es el consejero de la escuela, él atiende a toda la comunidad, y entonces él está saturado de trabajo, y pienso que no se toma la molestia, nomás nos manda una cartita, y antes de que yo llegara al correo esa carta ya no estaba allí, porque Diego la sacaba, firmaba, respondía...

E: Tú me dijiste algo interesante...me dices que los niños hispanos son problemáticos...decime más de eso...

P: Si los niños hispanos son, ah, yo lo note con Diego, cuando él llego de México aquí., apenas tenia nueve años, y yo veía como les, como la relación entre profesor-alumno, como que ya se frustraban y no hacían más...

E: Cuéntame. ¿Que habías visto?

P: Les decían, "Niños no hablen en español, puro inglés". Les decían (en inglés, claro), ellos (los niños) decían, "Yo no hablo inglés" y se sentaban en el suelo, se sentaban arriba de la mesa, de los bancos, donde escribían, y por mas que los maestros querían castigarlos, solo les daban sus cinco minutos de retención, media hora de retención. Diego me llegaba a veces con media hora de retención, "Eh ¿Por qué me llegaste tarde?"; "Ah, es que hablé en una clase, me regañaron, me dijeron que a la salida tenia media hora en la dirección, algo así..."

E: Ah, ¿After school detention... ?

P: Si, entonces, este, varios eran con ese problema, cuando iba Diego a esa escuela había muy pocos hispanos, creo que como, como cinco o seis con él, eran muy poquitos. Entonces, no les ponían *mano dura*, decían "no podemos con ellos", pero estos niños no iban tan mal, iban más o menos, iban súper en matemáticas...

E: ¿Eso fue en elementary o middle school?

P: Era quinto grado ¿Eso qué es?

E: Eso es elementary...

P: Elementary, okay, entonces de allí empezó todo esto y yo lo veía con él y con sus amigos, yo les decía que (el niño de tres años interrumpe la charla para pedir un popote). Yo les decía, "Ustedes no ponen atención a lo que les dicen". Y si, nosotros no, entonces yo veía este problema, en el deporte iban súper bien, este, en matemáticas iban súper bien, en historia iban mal y no les exigían, no ponían atención, ellos eran rebeldes, ellos eran rebeldes, y ahorita lo que yo vi, cuando Diego fue a la escuela, eh, en esta escuela que él estudió que estaba detrás de mi casa, ahí ya los niños ya usaban drogas, los hispanos, y los morenos...

E: ¿Nueve años me dijiste que tenían?

P: Si, pero no cuando él estudio, ahora que él estudió high school, y yo, yo visitaba la escuela, porque ahí tenía sobrinos, a los niños les encontraban drogas en sus lockers, o sea que ese, si, tienen nueve, diez, once años, hasta once grado en esa escuela, dije, "no, que bárbaro, esto esta tremendo..."

E: Aja...

P: Pero con Diego en esa escuela me imagino que era lo mismo, solo que, uno ni por enterado, pero ya son mayores, ya son de, de trece años a dieciséis y Diego de hecho cuando salió de ahí ya tenia diecisiete años...

E: Aja...

P: No se pudo hacer más para que siguiera estudiando...

E: Cuando me dijiste que él empezó acá el high school...

P: (Interrumpiendo). No. ¿Cuando él empezó a estudiar?

E: No, no, digo, cuando él empezó acá que empezaron todos estos problemas que tú me dices, que él no iba, que te falsificaba la firma. Cuéntame desde que empezó high school como fue hasta que tú te enteras de todo esto. ¿Fue en el primer año de high school?

P: No, no, fue casi medio año, después de seis meses que él empezó a hacer todo eso, si, porque, este, de hecho, él iba muy bien, y yo sabia que si no iba bien no podía estar en deporte...

E: Aja.

P: Entonces, él estaba en football americano, y le apasionaba, y entonces, y era buen jugador, entonces estaba perfecto, y todo estuvo muy bien en la escuela. Me imagino porque él continuaba en el deporte, de allí empezó mal y mal, y estaba en, en luchas greco-romanas. ¿Cómo le llaman wrestling?

E: Wrestling...

P: Wrestling, estaba en eso, y también le encantaba, porque en eso había estado en la elementary, y le encantaba...

E: O sea que ¿La misma escuela si él no andaba bien en los grados no lo dejaban participar en deportes o ustedes los padres... ?

P: (Interrumpiendo). No lo dejaban, no, la escuela, la escuela, si no cumples con tus grados no puedes hacer deportes. Entonces creo que empezó a bajar los grados, lo sacaron del football americano, se metió otra vez al wrestling, estuvo allí, y de allí, este, otra vez bajo, y lo sacaron. Él decía que él se salía, él aquí nos mentía y decía, "No, ya no me gusta eso, ya me voy de acá". Y se empezó a subir (los grados), entro al soccer y eso si lo apasiono, fue lo que más le encantaba...

E: Me acuerdo...

P: Entonces, ya de ahí fue peor su situación porque ya de ahí no se recuperaba de sus materias, ya estaba reprobando y bajando, y no lo aprobaban en sus créditos. Entonces ya de allí, este, en el football iba arriba, era el mejor goleador, el mejor jugador, este, y de allí dijeron, cuando le empezaron a investigar todos sus grados, que iba súper mal, y que no iba a clases. Entonces dijeron los del deporte, dijeron, "¿Sabes qué? Este niño está muy mal, lo siento, es el mejor jugador pero debido a esto nos van a anular todos los partidos que hemos ganado". O sea que la escuela, el equipo, y todo se vino abajo por Diego.

E: Ah...¿Le anularon los partidos?

P: Si, porque él era el goleador, él metía cuatro, tres, cinco goles por partido y eran con los que ganaban, entonces al él meter tres goles, y habían ganado tres a dos entonces eran cero a dos y ganaba el otro equipo, entonces empezaron a hacer un recuento de todo eso y dijeron, "No, ese niño, no" (pausa).

E: ¿O sea que la escuela tiene una regla que dice que si el niño no anda bien en los grados no puede participar en deportes?

P: No puede participar en deportes...

E: ¿Es así bien clarito?

P: Si, eso yo lo sabia desde que estaba en elementary, porque empezó a bajarme en elementary cuando tenia diez años, y empezó a bajarme porque las niñas le llamaban por teléfono y equis y él quería salir, no lo sacábamos, no lo dejábamos tampoco. Y, este, le dije, "Ah, este, ya me estás bajando, mira aquí me bajaste en historia y en esto y te me sales del deporte". Y ya como a las dos semanas no iba a practicar le digo, "¿Ya te saliste?"; No de todas maneras ya me sacaron dice porque como baje en este materia, y ahí no quieren de, de 70 (puntos) no, quieren de 85 (puntos) hacia arriba, entonces si tienes 70-80 (puntos) no puedes estar, y aquí en el high school eso fue con su, no, él traía la moral por los suelos, fue cuando ya estaba atendiéndose contigo, y este, y toda esa problemática, pero si, fue bastante frustrante, pero yo he visto en Diego que nada lo tumba, le duele en el momento, le duele su orgullo las cosas malas que le pasan, pero no aprende...

E: ¿No aprende?

P: No aprende...

E: ¿Por qué decís eso?

P: Porque, porque hace una tras otra, hace cosas que, que no están bien, y siento que, que él no aprende, que él no siente un dolor que, a lo mejor, bueno no se, él se crió desde niño muy fuerte porque yo lo hice muy fuerte, entonces él se hizo un niño muy fuerte criado con mis papás y conmigo, entonces, él, él deseaba algo y se le compraba...

E: Cuando decís "muy fuerte" decime más de eso. ¿A qué te referís con "muy fuerte"?

P: No, como que, él no era de los que les pasa algo y llora...

E: ¿Te referís al carácter?

P: De carácter fuerte si, de carácter, y siento que no, él cuando le pasan (cosas) malas él no llora, él no se desahoga, *él anda como un animalito enjaulado así como que, no se puede estar quieto*, anda buscando que, pero como enojado, como enojado, entonces no demuestra dolor, no demuestra pena, no demuestra tristeza, entonces él (pausa).

E: ¿Pero si demuestra enojo?

P: Si, enojo si...

E: ¿Y cómo lo demuestra?

P: Pues que si le habla uno fuerte o le reclama uno algo se enoja y contesta mal...y se le ve en sus acciones...

E: ¿Pero no lo has visto triste me quieres decir?

P: Si, casi nunca, casi nunca, y así cuando ha terminado con novias también no, no demuestra tristeza o dolor, que le digo, una vez cuando lo vi, sentí que sufrió mucho porque quería mucho a esa niña pero no lo demostraba. Le dije, "Ya viste, pero no andes haciendo cosas malas. ¿Cómo puedes andar con alguien que amas, y andas con otra, con otra niña? Entonces, no puedes jugar con los sentimientos de los demás". "Ay, no te metas, es mi vida, yo sé lo que hago" me dijo. Y, yo sé que le dolía, pero bueno, estaba enojado y no es que se calle, o diga, "Si mamá, yo cometí un error". No, no, él no reconoce casi nunca lo malo que hace...

E: ¿Y tú qué piensas de eso? ¿Has hablado con él o... ?

P: (Interrumpiendo). Si, hemos hablado mucho con él y no, yo siento que de sus experiencias él no aprende mucho, él no aprende mucho, entonces, es como me dice mi esposo, "Le van a pasar cosas, tras cosas, tras cosas, buenas y malas, y él va a seguir en las mismas". Entonces él va a madurar cuando ya sea grande, cuando tenga a sus hijos, porque a veces así pasa, uno no madura hasta que le pasa muchas cosas malas...

E: Claro es verdad...Y dime una cosa ¿Cómo fue la comunicación con la escuela cuando todo esto pasaba? Tú me dices que no te informaron porque las cartas que mandaban él las agarraba, o no llegaban a ti. ¿Cómo fue, nunca te llamaron, fuiste, hablaste con alguien?

P: No, ya de todo eso ya casi pasaron dos años de que, él curso bien seis meses, entre bien y mal otros seis meses que fue un año. Pero el segundo año empezó mal y hasta el tercer año de que estudio high school, este, ya iba súper mal. Entonces fue cuando yo me enteré, y fue cuando, fue el segundo año de, de que él hacia todo esto. Entonces pasaron dos años casi exactamente de que él ya, se salía de clases, no iba bien, no pasaba materias. Y se supone que debía de acreditar ya a lo mejor, ya veinte grados, y él llevaba nada más nueve, los del primer año que, que fue cuando estuvo bien. Entonces los demás no los acreditaba y él seguía pasando, seguía en otro grado, y en otro grado...

E: ¿Cómo es que pasaba de grado si no tenía los créditos?

P: Si, no lo entiendo...

E: ¿Y la escuela no te llamaba, no te decía, "Mire señora..."?

P: (Interrumpiendo). No, todo esto fue al final, le digo ya de hace dos años, entonces, eh, si, ya los dos años ya hemos hablado con el consejero y con todo un cabildo de, un juez, todo ellos. Y, ya ahí, este, yo no fui, fue mi esposo y, y fue Diego, y ya dijeron que él como tutor, tenia muchos problemas ya por la conducta de Diego. Entonces si Diego faltaba, ya le iban a cobrar 50 dólares por cada día que faltara Diego a la escuela, 50 dólares porque ya había sobrepasado los límites de las faltas.

E: ¿Cuántos días había faltado más o menos? ¿Lo recuerdas?

P: No, no recuerdo, pero, pues si un semestre tiene por decir así, si un semestre tiene 100 clases, él tenia, este, 40 clases asistidas y 60 no asistidas, entonces si ya era más del limite, y ya dijeron, "Ya no vamos a, ya el problema no es Diego, ya el problema son los papás de Diego".

E: ¿Quién dijo eso?

P: Eh, los de, los que estaban allí, no se quienes, era un (pausa larga).

E: ¿Dónde era eso en la escuela?

P: No, en la escuela, en otra...

E: ¿El consejo de educación?

P: Si, allí, ya, el consejo de educación...

E: Si, yo me acuerdo que tu esposo me contó que habían hecho una reunión, y una persona le dijo que el problema de Diego eran los padres.

P: Si, entonces, y nosotros le dijimos, "Bueno, pero si es la primera vez que me entero de todo esto que me están diciendo, yo no estaba enterado entonces ¿Cómo pueden hacer eso?"; Ellos dijeron, "No, es que usted no se enteró porque no pone atención con su hijo, pero ya ha pasado esto, esto, le hemos mandado cientos de cartas durante todo este tiempo, y ya tenía dos años, y han hecho caso omiso de las cartas". Bueno, pero tu tienes, y luego él (esposo) viene y me dice, "¿Tú te enteraste de estas cartas?" Y yo le dije, "Nunca las vi, nunca las leí, nunca las contesté porque nunca llegaron a mis manos". Entonces ya fue Diego que dijo, "No, es que yo las firmaba, yo las contestaba, yo llevaba a alguien a la escuela". Y, o sea, como todo eso pasa a ojos cerrados de nosotros los padres. Entonces dijeron, "Si ustedes ya no cumplen, o Diego sigue faltando, o se lleva a algún compañerito, o ustedes se van a la cárcel, o ustedes pagan 50 dólares por cada ausencia de Diego".

E: Aja...

P: No, ya bien enojado mi esposo, y a ponerle *mano dura* a Diego, y ya fue cuando estaba en atención con psicóloga y todo, que tú nos ayudaste, si se compuso en esa temporada, se compuso bastante pero...

E: ¿Lo mandaron a corte o no lo habían mandado a corte... ?

P: Si, lo mandaron a corte, lo mandaron a corte, de allí se fue a México, se fue a México, trató de estudiar allá...

E: ¿Ah se fue a México después que yo lo vi?

P: Si, si...

E: ¿Y cuánto tiempo estuvo en México... ?

P: Como dos meses...

E: Ah un tiempo corto...

P: No pudo estudiar...

E: ¿Por qué?

P: Porque no revalidaba materias, no tenia ninguna documentación, no, y aquí no logro sacar ningún documento, de, como que eso se tiene que hacer en el consulado, liberar la educación que lleva. Entonces ya él, pues fue frustrante también, no pudo hacer nada y se regresó, no estuvo ni dos meses, no se acostumbro...

E: ¿Dónde estuvo allá con tus padres?

P: Con mis papás, si, feliz porque lo adoran, y paseaba para allá y para acá pero...

E: Pero no pudo ir a la escuela...

P: La escuela no, y todo el mundo estaba en la escuela, entonces se aburría porque él estaba en la casa todo el tiempo...

E: ¿Decidió volver?

P: Y se regresó, este, a la corte fue mi esposo a apelar que él estaba en México, entonces como que quedó su caso cerrado...

E: Que bueno...

P: Cerrado, y él volvió, entonces ya luego de todo esto, una vez lo, iba para su trabajo al restaurante, y lo detuvieron, lo detuvo la policía porque iba a exceso de velocidad. Y le encontró todo su record otra vez, y se lo llevaron a encerrar a la cárcel detenido, y era menor de edad. Se supone, se supone que debían haber estudiado que sucedió con su caso, pero no lo estudiaron, entonces él estuvo ese día que era viernes, que iba a trabajar, estuvo todo el viernes desde las dos de la tarde, todo el viernes a la tarde, todo el sábado (pausa).

E: Porque justo fue un fin de semana...

P: Si, fue un fin de semana, y todo el domingo, el lunes por la mañana, y fuimos a hablar y dijeron que no podía salir, que hasta el lunes que lo vea la juez, pero él estaba en un cuarto detenido muy solo, no se si allí detengan a las personas, estaba solito en un cuarto...

E: ¿Aquí en la ciudad?

P: Si, aquí en la ciudad, en este condado, entonces el lunes hablaron a las siete de la mañana, habló la juez y que quería hablar con mi esposo. Y dijo, "No, si yo soy el tutor de Diego, soy su papá". Dicen, "Okay, tienen que venir por él". Mi esposo les pregunto si había que pagar algo o tenia que ir a la corte y le dijeron que tenía que venir por él inmediatamente. Y ya fue mi esposo por él y ya le dijeron que hablaron con Diego y que se disculpaban pero que Diego no debía de haber estado detenido...

E: ¿Cómo fue eso?

P: Pues porque no estudiaron su caso y su caso ya había estado cerrado.

E: ¿Y por qué lo detuvieron simplemente por exceso de velocidad?

P: Por exceso de velocidad y le encontraron su record anterior, pero el récord se supone que estaba cerrado, entonces, ya dijeron que, que se disculpaban pero que él nada mas debió de haber pasado, el viernes y salir en la noche, unas horas detenido. Se estudiaba su caso y salía y lo tuvieron sábado y domingo y entonces que no querían que él tomara represalias porque él podía demandar, Diego podía demandar por haber estado, por haberlo detenido. Entonces ya, dijo mi esposo, "¿Para qué buscarnos problemas si sabemos que tú traes problemas desde antes? Ya mejor no vamos a hacer nada, ya mejor pues vamos a la casa." Además que no le dejábamos que le metiéramos comida, no quisieron.

E: Cuando estuvo detenido...¿Ustedes le quisieron llevar algo para comer...?

P: Si, y ahí dijeron que no podíamos, pero un muchacho que estaba allí le llevó hamburguesas los dos días, él le llevo hamburguesas, y entonces Diego dice, "Yo no quería ni comer porque tenia el baño al lado de mi cama...¿Cómo iba a comer?" Entonces no quería comer, pero dice que si que se porto buena gente el muchacho y que decía que si quería fumar algo y él le dijo, "No, yo no fumo".

E: ¿Él estaba con otro muchacho en la misma...? **P: (Interrumpiendo). No, había alguien vigilándolo...E: Ah, alguien vigilándolo...¿Todo el tiempo?**

P: Si, ahí estuvo un muchacho de fin de semana, él y otra muchacha, entonces creo que cuando la muchacha se iba a descansar él se quedaba, y cuando él se iba a descansar ella se quedaba, en otro rato estaban juntos. Pero, este, siempre estuvo ahí alguien en esa oficinita, era una oficinita, una salita, y ya allí ese cuartito feo, allí, un baño, y una camita, entonces nosotros si fuimos a verlo, si nos permitieron verlo pero, ya luego la juez lo sacó antes de las 8:00 de mañana, antes de que se entraran a corte y todo eso, Diego salió, para que no hubiera problemas con ellos me imagino.

E: Que bueno, que bueno...

P: Y entonces ya lo trajo mi esposo le dijo, "Mira ¿Esto es lo que te gusta? ¿Eso quieres? No quieres escuela, no quieres trabajar, ¿Qué quieres?" Dice: "No, ya, yo iba a trabajar, sino que ya iba tarde, y le metí velocidad al carro y me pararon".

E: Entonces cuando él vino de México ¿Él no fue a la escuela él fue a trabajar?

P: Ya no fue a la escuela.

E: ¿Y qué edad tenía? ¿Me decís que era menor de edad?

P: Diecisiete...

E: ¿Por qué decidió que no iba a la escuela? ¿Por qué decidió ir a trabajar?

P: Ya no quiso, yo le busqué el programa para estudiar en casa, eh, el consejero me ayudó, aplicamos, y ya cuando me iban a mandar todo para que yo pagara, este, creo que iba a dar de inicio yo, 3.000 dólares, por un paquete de libros y estudiar en casa y este, ya teníamos computadora entonces le dijimos vas a estudiar aquí, y dice, "No, que yo no quiero, no gasten en mi, yo quiero trabajar, no voy a estudiar, voy a sacar mi GED (Examen para obtener un diploma de High School) no gasten en mi".

E: ¿Ese programa en qué consistía? ¿Era como home school?

P: Si home school...

E: Aja, ¿Y viene un paquete con libros y tú puedes preparar las materias solo?

P: Si, él puede estudiar solo, en casa, y sus exámenes son por computadora...

E: ¿Y depende de la escuela, depende de la secretaria de educación, o es algo aparte?

P: Creo que es algo aparte, pero es del gobierno, del estado, pero es como un programa para niños que quieran estudiar en la casa.

E: ¿Y hay que tener un motivo por el cual uno elige ese programa o uno simplemente porque quiera estudiar ya se lo dan?

P: Pues, a veces, cuando, como él que ya era un "niño problema", entonces dijeron, "puedes estudiar en tu casa", si porque, ya no quería, ya iba a cumplir la, entonces la escuela dijo, "Pues yo ya no lo quiero aquí porque ya".

E: Pero la escuela nunca lo llegó a expulsar ¿O si lo expulsaron? ¿Ni tampoco suspendido?

P: No, nunca, suspendido si, pero ni nos enterábamos...

E: Pero no suspendido en la escuela, me refiero a suspendido en la casa. ¿Fue suspendido?

P: Si, si, supongo que si, si lo suspendían pero él ni venia a la casa, ni nos enterábamos, ni sabia que estaba suspendido porque mejor se iba de pinta, pero si, si lo suspendían, también lo tenían en la dirección detenido ahí por horas.

E: ¿Y tú alguna vez fuiste a la escuela, has hablado, con quién hablaste cuando fuiste? No me digas el nombre, pero digo ¿El principal? ¿El maestro?

P: Una principal, el principal era un hombre, y la segunda, ella, y fue cuando yo lo vi allá detenido. Le dije a mi esposo, "Vamos a ver como va Diego" y fuimos a ver. Dicen, no, dicen, eso tenia casi como seis meses de problemas. Dice, "No, Diego, pues no va muy mal, pero, este, no va muy bien en sus materias y queremos que le pongan atención y mire, él va muy bien en el deporte, él tiene muchos amigos, es un niño muy popular, aquí todos lo quieren mucho, los maestros hablan muy bien de él". Le digo, "Bueno, pero que lo quieran mucho, se lleven bien con él, no quiere decir que él vaya bien en la escuela, no porque te estimen mucho y te quieran mucho, y eres un buen niño, te voy a pasar de grado si tú no vienes a mi clase". Entonces él pensaba que a lo mejor de esa manera iba a pasar grados que se llevaba súper con sus maestros.

E: Claro, o sea que tú hablaste con esta persona. ¿Y cómo fue? ¿Tú hablas inglés?

P: No...

E: ¿Cómo fue? ¿Tienen intérprete, hablan en español, cómo es la comunicación?

P: No, en inglés, todo fue en inglés.

E: ¿Y tú les entendías?

P: No, yo no, mi esposo habla inglés.

E: Ah tu esposo habla inglés..

P: Si, él hablaba inglés.

E: Claro. ¿Ellos no proveen un intérprete para los papás que no hablan inglés?

P: Supongo que si, pero en ese momento no pedimos, no nos trajeron, y ya.

E: Ah, okay.

P: Entonces, este, ya cuando lo íbamos a sacar de la escuela, también después de que paso todo eso, que hablamos con el consejero y ya, fui con mi esposo y hablamos, ya con varias personas, porque ya querían que les dijéramos, que ya él ya iba a venirse de la escuela, o sea Diego ya no va a venir a la escuela, ya no va a estudiar aquí, va a estar en un programa de home school...

E: ¿Ellos querían que tú le digas eso?

P: Yo pienso, porque tampoco yo lo podía sacar, no tenía la edad para sacarlo, él iba a cumplir diecisiete años, tenía que seguir en la escuela. Dicen, "Bueno, después de las vacaciones, él ya tiene dieciocho años, ya tiene dieciocho años pero no, no puede irse antes".

E: Ah, claro, tenía que seguir hasta los dieciocho años.

P: Aja, entonces, les dijimos a ellos, luego nos mandaron al piso de abajo, fuimos a hablar con otro, porque yo, yo quería que él siguiera allí, aunque él tuviera la edad. Y dijo, "Él, mire, ya no es ningún problema que esté aquí, si él quiere y promete que va a cumplir, está bien, pero ya no tiene caso, cuando ya tenga dieciocho años ya no tiene caso que él esté aquí". Entonces (dijeron ellos), "Es mejor que si ustedes le van a poner ese programa en su casa, que estudie, y exíjanle, y cuídenlo, y véanlo, porque va a estar en su casa, entonces él va a estudiar y va a hacer sus trabajos, y ustedes van a estar seguros de que lo está haciendo, y no se está yendo de pinta, porque ustedes están en casa". Entonces dijeron, "Por nosotros no hay ningún problema, si él quiere estudiar, quiere venir, pero que venga a estudiar, no que venga a jugar o a pasear.

E: Claro.

P: Entonces dijeron, "Bueno, si ustedes quieren eso, está bien, pero si le tienen su programa está mejor, que estudie en su casa, no lo estamos corriendo, pero si ya no podemos con él, y ustedes no pueden con él, entonces hay que tomar medidas más drásticas, él ya tiene corte y tiene que ir a cumplir a su corte". Entonces ya de ahí, si lo llevamos a una corte, tenia varias, lo llevamos a una, y ahí si, una juez me regaño horriblemente a mí, lo regaño a él. Y dijo, le dijo a él, le dijo, "Mira, tu mamá es mexicana, no es ciudadana, es una ilegal, tu papá es un ilegal, ustedes no deben estar en este país, y tú todavía no quieres estudiar. ¿Sabes que puedo hacer yo? Mandarte a tu país, con tu mamá y tu papá". Diego le dijo, "Pero ellos tienen trabajo aquí". "¿Qué tienen?", le pregunto (la juez). "No, que tienen un negocio así, acá, de comida", (dijo él). Ella dijo, "Pues yo les puedo quitar su negocio, les puedo quitar todo y se van a su país, y se van con los brazos cruzados. ¿Tu quieres eso?"

E: ¿El juez dijo eso?

P: Si, yo pienso que lo hizo a manera de que Diego agarrara conciencia ¿no? Por tu culpa tus padres se pueden largar de aquí, y sin nada, y les quitamos todo. Le dice, "¿Tu quieres eso para tu mamá y tu papá?". "No, que no" (dijo él). "Bueno, pues entonces quiero que tomes conciencia, y que si vas a ir a la escuela vas a ir a estudiar, y si no vas a ir a la escuela vas a estar estudiando en tu casa, pero que ya no andes incitando a otros que vayan de pinta contigo". El niño dice, "Bueno, yo no los obligo, yo nunca obligué a nadie, todos se fueron conmigo cuando querían, a veces yo no quería y ellos querían y yo los llevaba". La juez dijo, "Bueno, pero a ti tampoco nadie te obliga, por eso tu fuiste un mal niño porque quisiste ser un mal niño, pero si quieres eso para tus papás, hacemos eso". Y ya lo regañaron a él y me regañaron a mí, ya salimos de ahí. Y yo le dije, "¿Ya viste?" Yo también dándole a él, ya salimos de ahí, y esa vez creo que nada mas pagué 110 dólares, y ya salimos de allí, le dieron otra corte para ver.

E: El motivo de la corte siempre era por los días que él había perdido de escuela ¿verdad? No había otros motivos.

P: No...

E: ¿Él nunca tuvo problemas con drogas, ni con alcohol, o mala conducta?

P: No, nunca, ni golpearse con nadie...

E: ¿O sea que él no tenía un mal comportamiento? ¿Lo único era que él no iba a la escuela?

P: No, no iba a clase, entonces cuando te dicen no vas a clase, pues es porque, estás enfermo, o tus papás te requieren que los vayas a interpretar a algún lado, o porque te hacen trabajar, pero no...

E: No era el caso...

P: No, de hecho él ni trabajaba, y cuando tenía que trabajar decía, "No, no puedo ayudarlos porque tengo que ir a la escuela". Y nosotros creyendo que iba a la escuela le decíamos, "No, si tienes que estudiar, vete a la escuela". Pero, este, de hecho él no era, no tenia ni mal comportamiento, ni era grosero, ni drogas, ni alcohol.

E: Y cuando tú me dices que le dieron carro, le dieron celular, le dieron cierta libertad. ¿Tu qué piensas de eso, ahora, mirando para atrás digamos?

P: Pues, es lo que le decimos a él, le digo, "Mira Diego, hicimos un mal dándote todo, porque gracias a eso, tu empezaste a errar tu camino, a agarrar por otro camino malo". Él dice, "No, pero es que, estaba bien, solo que yo con los cuates, porque queríamos ser más, diferentes a los demás, entonces hacíamos otras cosas". Él dice, "Pero de hecho no estuvo mal, yo, yo nunca lo use para drogas, nunca lo use para alcohol, era para gasolina y para comida lo que me daban, el celular, ustedes me localizaban y yo les decía, 'No, estoy practicando football, o estoy en el soccer, o estoy acá', y el vehiculo, pues yo lo agarraba para ir a la escuela". Pero en realidad no era para ir a la escuela. Y es lo que le digo a mi esposo, "Hicimos muy mal porque le dimos todo, como que, como que lo compramos con dinero y con todo, para que él estuviera bien, pero pensamos que él iba bien en la escuela". Nosotros lo estábamos premiando por el estudio, y porque ya no podíamos llevarlo a la escuela ni traerlo, entonces dijimos, "Bueno que tenga vehiculo, que tenga celular, que tenga dinero". Pero ahora que veo las cosas, mi esposo me dice que no hicimos mal, yo pienso que hicimos muy mal. Le digo, "Si, hicimos muy mal, porque los niños cuando desean las cosas a lo mejor las quieren, y se esperan a que tengan, o uno como padre se espera a que tengan cierta edad, y les dan las cosas, o cuando tú veas el resultado de lo que tú quieres le das su premio, y nosotros no vimos nada y le dimos premio".

E: ¿Y él pidió esas cosas o ustedes se las dieron sin que él las pida?

P: No, él pidió, él dijo, "No, miren, ya no me quiero ir en el bus, luego, hay un chavo ahí, la vez pasada me quería pelear con él, porque es problemático, y no se que". Era un "bolillo" (Bolillo es una especie de pan mexicano. En el lunfardo mexicano, es un término para referirse a los americanos blancos, en referencia a los panes mexicanos de color blanco), un americano. Y dijo, "Ya no me quiero ir a mi escuela, este, y además el bus pasa bien temprano, una hora antes de que yo llegue a mi clase, y este, pues ando una hora paseando por la ciudad, mejor". Y teníamos un vehiculo aquí, ya lo teníamos al carro, no le compramos exclusivamente, lo teníamos parado. Él dijo, "¿Por qué no me dan el carro para que vaya a la escuela, y llegue mas temprano al trabajo, y así les ayude?" Le dijimos "okay", entonces le dimos carro, y, este, y a mi se me había descompuesto un celular en ese entonces, y tuvimos otro, y ya luego ese logró andar. Y él dijo, "Ese celular, ¿Por qué no me dan el celular que tenía mi mamá?" "Bueno agarralo", y ya tenía (pausa).

E: Fue como una sucesión de cosas…un proceso…

P: Si, fue un proceso así de, no fue de que dijimos, "Ah, ya, hay dinero, ten un carro, ten un celular".

E: Claro, él fue pidiendo, ustedes lo tenían, y fueron como negociando ¿verdad?

P: Exactamente, entonces, este, pues, pues él nos ayudaba con el niño, cuando estábamos bien entregados con el trabajo y bien llenos de gente, bien ocupados, él podía jugar con su hermanito, ir, salirse ahí a un área donde no había carros y entretenerlo, o tenía televisión en la camioneta, en la camioneta se estaban, y ahí se estaba entretenido con él, y de cierta manera nos ayudaba. Nunca nos ha gustado dar a cuidar a los niños, a nadie los hemos dado a cuidar, yo siempre, de hecho, yo inclusive, antes yo cuidaba niños, pero yo digo, "No, como yo los cuido, no los va a cuidar otra persona". Y se ven tantas cosas feas que nunca lo hemos hecho y él atendía a su hermanito, después de clases él venia, y era la ayuda que nos daba, atendía a su hermanito. O le decíamos, "Oye, llévale sodas a aquellos clientes, necesitan sodas". Les llevaba soda, y así era la ayuda que él nos daba, él no se metía de hecho a hacer, a trabajar…

E: Dime una cosa. ¿Recuerdas alguna situación que fuiste a la escuela a hablar, algún otro contacto con la escuela? ¿Hablaste con alguien, llamaban por teléfono, te mandaban

por ejemplo eso que le llaman "report card" (boletín) con las notas, con los grados, cómo era la comunicación con la escuela?

P: No, yo solo fui, de hecho, en su high schoool, solo estuve allí como cuatro veces, dos veces para inscribirlo a él, y otras dos para hablar ya cuando, una vez que nos hablaron ya con los problemas, y fuimos con varias personas, y la última vez cuando ya fuimos a hablar con varias personas para decirles que ya lo íbamos a sacar de la escuela para que estudiara en casa. En cuatro ocasiones yo estuve en la escuela, y las demás fueron por el deporte, yo iba a verlo jugar, y estábamos en la escuela, él jugaba en su escuela, pero fueron las únicas veces que yo tuve contacto con personas así, y todo fue en inglés, nunca me buscaban una intérprete.

E: ¿Nunca pediste una intérprete, nunca te lo ofrecieron, o...?

P: (Interrumpiendo). Nunca pedí, nunca me ofrecieron, fue un, un trato muy breve con la escuela, como padre, siento que no fue, no tuve trato con la escuela...

E: ¿Y por qué tú crees eso? ¿Por qué paso eso? ¿Tú no lo buscaste demasiado, ellos no te llamaban, como, o las dos cosas? ¿Cuál fue el motivo?

P: Pues, yo no, sentía que yo no necesitaba ir a la escuela porque si él iba bien, yo ya no hacía nada, hacía caso omiso de como fuera él. Cuando ya hubo los problemas, Diego se encargaba de todo eso y yo ni enterada estaba, él firmaba, llevaba notas, llevaba reportes, pero yo ni enterada estaba, ni el papá, porque él si, él se enojaba o algo y decía, "No, yo voy a ir a la escuela, voy a ir a preguntar como vas". El niño decía, "No, muy bien, aquí están mis grados, y nos daba los grados".

E: ¿Cómo estaban los grados?

P: Y los grados, había, pues fue el primer año, todo el primer año y parte del otro medio año, que iba bien, y ya de los demás grados jamás los mostró. Y yo decía, "¿Y la boleta?" Y él decía, "Ah, ya me la dieron, pero ya la devolví otra vez porque tiene uno que devolverla". Y ya nunca las volvíamos a ver, y no sabíamos como salía, sino que cuando yo lo iba a inscribir, sino que solo decían, "No, que firme aquí, él va a tomar estas y estas materias, va a repetir estas". Y ya, pero, pero nunca fue así de que yo me adentrara, además no me gustaba a mí ir por el idioma, porque ni me buscaban, nadie me ofrecía intérprete, ni me buscaban intérprete, yo tenía ahí que entenderles que me decían...

E: ¿Y tú no te animabas a decirles, "necesito un intérprete o me sentiría más cómoda si me consiguen un intérprete?"

P: No, porque fueron dos ocasiones para inscribirlo, dos ocasiones para ir a hablar con ellos, iba con mi esposo, y si una que otra vez lo necesité para llevarlo al doctor, y yo iba y le decía, "Necesito, este, hablar con Diego". Ya lo buscaban, decían, "A Diego lo busca su mamá". Y ya firmábamos y si nos teníamos que ir, firmaba yo y ya nos íbamos, luego lo regresaba o ya le decía, "Ya no va a regresar", y ya era todo. Pero nunca fue que yo fuera a buscar información ni nada, y mi esposo tampoco nunca se metió, cuando mis amigas empezaron a tener problemas con sus hijos, yo digo, "No, Diego no tiene problemas". Y a lo mejor ellas sabían que si y no me lo decían. Le digo, "No, Diego ahí va a la escuela, no va perfecto, pero está yendo a la escuela y bien". Pero nunca me adentré a investigar más, y fue un error bien grande, con mi otro hijo no lo voy a hacer, no, con él, no entiendo el idioma pero yo voy y le digo, "Dile a tu maestra esto, dile que quiero saber como vas".

E: Tú puedes solicitar un intérprete, tú tienes derecho a solicitar un intérprete.

P: En su escuela no lo hay pero me imagino que lo ponen por teléfono.

E: Pienso que si tienes derecho a un intérprete, en un hospital, en una escuela, es tu derecho.

P: Si, en su escuela hay muy poquitos hispanos, aquí donde él va hay como diez, entonces...

E: Pero igual aunque haya uno tienen que tener intérprete porque los padres por ahí no hablan el idioma ¿Verdad?

P: Si, igual yo no me estoy dejando con él, yo estoy mucho sobre él, sobre él, sobre él. Está sobresaliendo bastante, va muy bien en la escuela, tiene sus reconocimientos y pues, digo, no voy a quedarme como con Diego, porque ya tuve una mala experiencia, y si me frustro, porque yo siento que si hubiera hecho más, a lo mejor él hubiera terminado su high school, pero él dice que no, que de todas maneras la escuela no se hizo para él.

E: Ah, okay.

P: A él no le gusta la escuela, que nunca le ha gustado la escuela, tenía amigas y todas han salido mal, de todas sus calificaciones han salido mal, y decían que solo iban a calentar la banca a la escuela, pero todos lograron sacar su GED, mal, peor, como iban, horriblemente, pero tienen su GED de high school, le digo y él no.

E: Bueno, por ahí en algún momento se decide y lo saca ¿Verdad?

P: Si, exactamente, yo si tengo mucha ilusión de que él saque su GED, y quisiera que él estudiara algo, el papá ya fue a investigar ahí en el tecnológico y dice que él puede estudiar, con su GED, él puede estudiar una carrera técnica de electromecánica, de ingeniería...

E: Que bueno...¿Y él quisiera?

P: No, él no quiere, ya le dijimos, "Te pagamos tus estudios, vas a tener tus gastos", no quiere.

E: Le gusta trabajar...¿Decidió trabajar?

P: Pues, según él, también se cansa, a veces se aburre...

E: Bueno, puede cambiar de idea es muy jovencito, y dime una cosa, ¿Cuáles son tus expectativas como mamá para él, que te gustaría para él?

P: Bueno, yo como toda mamá soñadora, yo quisiera que él se casara, que tuviera su familia, y al menos que tuviera una carrera técnica, corta pero que tuviera algo en que defenderse aquí, porque de por si, si no tiene uno seguro social, si no tenemos ninguna documentación de que podamos estar bien en el país, somos un don nadie ¿Verdad? Y sin estudios tantito peor, a él le ayuda muchísimo que habla inglés, y es un niño muy carismático, tiene, tiene muy, un don de gente que (pausa).

E: Es muy agradable...

P: Si, la gente lo atiende bien donde sea, americanos, hispanos, pero yo quisiera que, pues, que él creciera más como ser humano, y que pudiera lograr aunque sea una carrera corta, ahora ya va a ser papá, tiene su novia, la chica está embarazada, ellos se independizaron, viven juntos, pagan sus gastos. Le digo, "Bueno, eso está perfecto, pero me agradaría que te casaras con ella".

E: Dime un poco de eso, no conozco, yo soy de Argentina ¿Es importante para ustedes casarse, vivir juntos, cómo es eso en la cultura de ustedes?

P: La cultura de nosotros, pues, es que si ya te casas, ya cumples con tu pareja y puedes estar con ella todo el tiempo, pero ya con las leyes de Dios y las leyes de los papeles, si, porque así amparas a tus hijos. Si de cierta manera, en algún momento te separas, tus hijos quedan desamparados y sin un papá, pero si tienes papeles, tú tienes ya el apellido de tu padre, de tu madre y de un matrimonio bien, porque sino somos hijos naturales, solo eres hijo de la mamá, te ponen el apellido y todo de la mamá. Entonces, si, en nuestra cultura es muy bueno que uno esté casado, que uno esté, tenga sus documentos como pareja, y así quedan amparados los hijos. Si tú faltas, si el padre falta, los hijos tienen derecho a ciertas cosas que el padre tiene, y sino pues, un buen apellido y que es un hijo de matrimonio, pero, este, él se hizo a la idea de liberalismo americano...

E: Dime más de eso...

P: Pues es él como los americanos, él dice, "No, yo no necesito un papel yo no me quiero casar, ya estoy con ella". La chica también dice, "No, si ahorita nos queremos y al rato no nos queremos, cada quien por su lado".

E: ¿Y tú crees que los americanos hacen eso?

P: No, no creo...

E: ¿Por qué me decís que se hizo a la idea americana... **?** **Porque los americanos yo veo que se casan, les gusta casarse**...

P: ¿Si?

E: Me parece...

P: Pero los niños de escuela con los que él estudió, son compañeros de 17-18 años, tienen sus novias, las embarazan y se van, y al rato andan con otra, y ellas al rato andan con otro, no viven juntos, y los bebés los tienen las abuelas, yo así vi con él, de cuando él estudiaba, y él no lo hizo, pero salió de la escuela y ahorita ya está...

E: Ah, yo pensé que vos hablabas de vivir juntos sin casarse, eso es más Hispano...

P: Si, si, de hecho, si lo hacen eso, los hispanos viven en unión libre la mayoría...

E: Viven en unión libre, y por ahí pasan 20, 30 años y viven juntos...

P: Si, pero también se ve mucho de que si viven en unión libre pueden dejarse y se juntan con otra persona y...

E: Puede ser, puede ser...

P: Y los hijos bien gracias, y luego hay un montón de niños con diferente papá y mamá y así, y los americanos yo veo muchos también, aunque estén casados, que están con otra persona, los hispanos somos más conservadores, la familia es más tradicional. La familia de mi esposo si son de que uno se casa, la mía también, aquí hay de todo tipo, de todas partes del mundo, y hay gente que nada más le gusta vivir en unión libre, pero a mi no me parece...

E: ¿No te parece?

P: No me parece, ahorita se lo dijimos a Diego, él pidió la mano de la novia, ellos estuvieron juntos cuatro años.

E: ¿Algo más que me quieras contar?

P: No, ya te dije todo (risas).

E: ¡Muchas gracias por tu tiempo!

P: ¡De nada y cualquier cosa que necesites aquí estamos!

E: ¡Muchas gracias!

APPENDIX 2

INTERVIEW
Interview #7—English

Mexican married mother with three children (ages 19, 8 and 3). Mother is monolingual (Spanish). She immigrated to the US in 1999. Parents are self-employed. Parents and oldest child are undocumented; two younger children are born in the US. Oldest child is a high school dropout. Mother described big problems to communicate with the school and the community in general.

Interviewer: Tell me about your experience as a mother of a child in high school...

Participant: I was very involved in my kid's problems because, actually, Diego started perfectly fine, we demanded him a lot, when he just started high school, our store started getting a lot of time and energy from us, so we neglected our responsibility about demanding Diego, like grades, and study. So, as the store was growing, I mean, he was given a car to go to school, he did not take the bus, and all our problems started from there, because he was given a cell phone to communicate with us, we spent less time with him, our little child was always with us. So it was *catastrophic*, the beginning of our store, because there was money to get more things, so we neglected his school. Our younger little boy did not go to school at that time, but Diego went to school. So he started driving, he started having money, he started using his cell phone, he had his friends in his car, and he did not go to class. I mean, when he went to class he was a very well behaved kid. Everybody liked him, they saw him achieving things and all that, but when he said "I am not going to school today I am going out." He would go out with his friends, he would say, "Hey, I have money, let's go, I take you to that city, let's go to that other city, let's go there...", and he would go out with a bunch of five or six friends.

I: Uh-huh...

P: So, the school did not communicate with me, they did not tell me anything about that, or they did, they asked him to tell me and he did not say anything to me, I did not know anything until a year and a half after all those problems started, I did not know anything (pause).

I: Uh-huh, you did not know anything...

P: No, and I thought my son was doing fine, I asked him, "How are you doing Diego?" He said, "I am doing fine, I have a grade that may be a little low but I will be okay." And we believed him, dad, mom, we all believed him (pause).

I: Uh-huh.

P: But it was so horrible when, I mean, the disappointment when, it was like two years later when I found out (pause).

I: How did you find out?

P: I found out because, some friends told me, I did not find out through the school, because, I believe Diego faked my signature, and when they (the school staff) asked him to go with his mom, he asked some of my friends to go to the school, and he told them (school staff) they (my friends) were his aunts and they signed for me, well (pause).

I: Did the school tell you?

P: No, Diego told me later, he told me that one of my friends went to school for her daughter, and he told my friend, "Look, my mom is working, you know, she is pregnant, she has a lot of problems with the baby, would you mind signing something for me? They are going to tell you something about me, but I am going to be there." She (my friend) told him, "Oh, yes, Diego, of course, tell your mom I said hello ok?" And she signed, and I believe that Diego faked my signature before that, he signed all the documents they sent me, he, he signed, and when he wanted to get permission to skip school, he signed, he would write a letter saying I wanted them to excuse him to miss school.

I: And the school never said anything?

P: The school is okay with that, I feel that the school does not apply a *mano dura* (firm hand) with Hispanics and with Hispanic's problems, because the Hispanic child is problematic. The Hispanic child in himself is problematic, so they (the teachers) would say "shut up" or "sit down," but they (the kids) would answer in Spanish. Sometimes they do not want to pay attention or they do not care about what they are told. I feel they are happy when they (the kids) are in ELL (English Language Learners) classes with other Hispanic kids. They have a great time there, a lot of fun (pause).

I: You mean the kids or the teachers?

P: No, the kids, students, teachers have no control, they cannot demand more than that to them, because we Hispanics work a lot. Americans understand their language, a phone call from the teacher, or the principal, or anybody. A phone call to a dad and that is perfect, but we do not, we must go with somebody else. Like the school counselor, we have in town, but he is overwhelmed with his job, I think he does not even bother himself to do anything. He would just send a little letter, and the letter was gone before I went to get it, because Diego took it, signed it, and sent it back to school (pause).

I: You said something very interesting before. You said that the Hispanic child is problematic. Say more about that...

P: Yes, Hispanic children are, um, I noticed that with Diego, when he first came from Mexico here, he was just nine years old, and I saw how they, I saw the teacher-student relationship. I saw them (teachers) getting very frustrated and giving up (pause).

I: Say more about that. What did you see?

P: They told them, "Do not speak in Spanish; speak in English." They said that in English of course, and the kids said, "I do not speak English." They were sitting on the floor, on their desks. Even though the teachers wanted to punish them, they just gave them after school detention for five minutes, or half an hour. Diego came home sometimes, like half an hour later and I asked him, "Hey, why are you coming late?" and he said, "Oh, I just talked in a class and they gave me a 30 minute after school detention at the principal office or whatever."

I: He was in after school detention... ?

P: Yes, so, um, a lot of kids had that problem, when Diego went to school, there were a few Hispanics, I believe there were like five or six Hispanic children with him, just a few, so, they did not apply a *mano dura* (firm hand). They said "We cannot handle them" but they (children) were not that bad, they were a little bad, they were very good at math (pause).

I: That was in elementary or middle school?

P: That was in fifth grade...is that elementary?

I: Yes, that is elementary school...

P: Elementary, okay, so everything started from there and I saw him and his friends. I told them (the 3 y/o child interrupts the conversation asking for a straw). I told him, "You do not pay attention to what they say." If we do not, so I saw that problem. In sports, they were great, um, in math, they were great, and in history, they were bad. They (teachers) did not demand anything, they (children) did not pay attention, they were rebellious, and what I saw, when Diego was in school, um, in the school he went, the school was behind my house and kids there use drugs, Hispanics and African Americans (pause).

I: Are you talking about the school he went when he was 9 years old?

P: Yes, it was not when he was in that school. It was now, when he was in high school, and I, I visited that school, because I have some nephews there, and they found drugs in the children's lockers, I mean, those children are nine, ten, eleven years old, they go to eleven grade in that school, I said, "Oh mine, that is terrible..."

I: Uh-huh...

P: But, with Diego in that school, I imagine it was the same, and I did not even know anything. They were older, they were from thirteen years old to sixteen years old, and actually Diego was seventeen years old when he left that school (pause).

I: Uh-huh...

P: We could not do anything else to make him stay in school...

I: When he started high school here...

P: (Interrupting) Are you asking when he started studying?

I: No, I mean, when he started going to school, when he had all those problems you mentioned before (he did not go to school, he faked your signature)...Tell me since he started high school, what happened until you found out, did it happened in his first year?

P: No, no, that was almost half a year after, six months after he started high school, yes, because, um, actually, he was doing very well, and I knew that if he were not doing well in school they would not have let him play sports (pause).

I: Uh-huh..

P: So, he was in football, American football, he was passionate about that, so, he was a good player so everything was *perfect*. I imagine everything was *great* at school because he was playing he was doing sports. He started having problems; he was in those luchas greco-romanas (wrestling) what is the name of that? Is it wrestling?

I: Wrestling...

P: Wrestling, he was doing that, and he loved that too because he did that in elementary school and he loved it (pause).

I: So are you saying that if he is not doing well in school, they will not let him participate in sports, or the parents decide that?

P: (Interrupting). They do not let him, the school, the school, if you do not have good grades, you cannot play sports, so I believe he started having bad grades, and they did not let him play football. He started doing wrestling again. He was there, um, his grades went down again, so they took him away, he said he left, he lied to me and said, "No, I do not like that anymore, I am going to quit that." Then, his grades were fine, and he started playing soccer, and he loved it, it was something he really loved (pause).

I: I remember that...

P: So, that was the worst situation ever because he could not get any credits, he failed all his classes, his grades went down. He did not get any credits, so from there, um, he was doing great in soccer, he was the top player, the best goal maker. He was the best player, um, and they (the school) said, they started investigating his grades, they found out that he was doing really bad, and he missed a lot of school days, so they told him, they said, "You know what? This kid is not doing well in school, I am sorry, he is the top soccer player but because of his academic problems we are going to invalidate all the games we won." So the school, the soccer team and everything went down because of him.

I: So they invalidated all the games.

P: Yes, because he was the goal maker, he made four, three, five goals in each game. They won the games, so if he made three goals, and they won like three-two they would count that like zero-two and the other team won. They started counting that and they said, "No, this kid is not going to be part of this."

I: So are you saying that the school has a rule that says that if a kid is not making progress or doing well academically they cannot participate in sports?

P: He cannot participate in sports...

I: Is it that explicit?

P: Yes, I already knew that since he was in elementary school, because he started having problems with his grades when he was ten years old, and his grades were not good, because the girls called him and all that and he wanted to go out. We did not let him go out, we did not take him anywhere either, and um, I told him, "Oh, um, your grades are getting lower, look at this grade in history and that other one, you are not going to play sports." Two weeks after that I asked him, "Are you playing sports?" He said, "They do not let me play sports anyway because of my grades." And they do not want them to have 70's, no, they want 85 or higher than that, so if you have 70-80 you cannot be there. Here in this high school, that was with his. No, um, he was very depressed. It was when you started seeing him, when he was in counseling with you, um, with all those problems. But, yes, it was very frustrating, but I have seen in Diego that nothing would take him down, he may be hurt for a while, his pride hurts when something bad happens, but he does not learn anything from that.

I: **He does not learn**...

P: He does not learn...

I: **Why do you say that?**

P: Because, because, he makes one mistake after another, he does things that are, that are not right. I feel like he does not learn, he does not feel pain, that, I mean, well, I do not know, he was raised as a strong kid, because, I made him very strong, so he was a strong kid raised by my parents and myself. So, if he wanted something, we would buy it for him...

I: **When you say "very strong"...say more about that...what do you mean by "very strong"?**

P: No, like, he is not one of those kids that something happens and they would cry...

I: **Do you mean that he has a strong personality?**

P: Yes, strong personality, personality, I feel like he does not, when something goes wrong he does not cry, he does not show his emotions, *he goes like a little animal in a cage,* like he cannot be still, he is looking for something, like angry, so he cannot show pain, sorrow, sadness, so he (pause).

I: **So you are saying that he can show anger**...

P: Yes, anger, yes...

I: **How does he show his anger?**

P: Um, if we yell at him or if we ask him to do something, he would be mad and give me a bad answer, you can tell by his actions (pause).

I: **And you said you don not see him sad...is that what you mean?**

P: Yes, I almost never, I almost never see him sad, and even when he broke up with girlfriends he did not show sadness or pain. I tell him, one time I saw him, I felt like he was suffering a lot over a girl, but he was not showing anything. I told him, "You see what happened, do not you do bad things, how can you be in a relationship with somebody you love and seeing another girl? You cannot play with people's emotions." He said, "Oh that is none of your business I know what I am doing." I knew he was suffering from that, but he was angry, he would never say, "Yes, mom, I made a mistake." No, no, he never admits his own mistakes.

I: What do you think about that? Have you tried to talk with him or...?

P: Yes, we had talked with him a lot, I do not, I do not feel that he learns much from his own experiences, he does not learn much. It is like, my husband says, "Things are going to happen to him, one after another, good and bad things, and he is going to do the same things, he will not mature until he gets older, until he has his own children, because, sometime that happens, one will not mature until a lot of bad things happen..."

I: True...Let me ask you something, how was the communication between you and the school when all this happened? You said the school did not contact you, I mean, they sent you letters but Diego intercepted them, so how was that, have they ever called you? Did you go to the school? Did you talk with anybody?

P: No, two years after all that happened, the first semester in high school was good. The second semester was okay, neither good nor bad, but the second year was bad until the third year. Um, so, when I found out he was doing bad, that was the second year, he did not go to school, he did not have any credits. He was supposed to have, like, twenty credit hours and he only had like nine credit hours, the ones he got in his first year. He passed to the next grade, the next grade, and the next grade (pause).

I: So he passed grades even though he did not have enough credits.

P: Yes, I do not understand that...

I: The school did not call you, did not say like "Look... ma'am"...?

P: (Interrupting). No, this was at the very end, after two years, so, um, we went to a meeting, we talked with a counselor and with a whole bunch of people, a judge, all of them. So then, I did not go to that meeting, my husband and Diego went to that meeting. And they (school staff) told him (husband) that he was not a good guardian and if Diego continued to miss school days, he (husband) was going to have to pay fifty dollars a day, because he missed too many school days...

I: Do you remember how many days he missed?

P: No, I do not remember, but if a semester has, let's say, if a semester has a hundred classes, he attended forty classes, and missed sixty classes, So, yes, he crossed the limit, and they said, "This is not Diego's problem, this is Diego's parents' problem."

I: Who said that?

P: Um, the, the people who attended that meeting, I do not know who they were...

I: Was that at the school?

P: No, it was not at the school, in another...

I: The board of education?

P: Yes, there, the board of education...

I: I remember that your husband told me there was a meeting at the BOE and somebody told him that he had a problem...

P: Yes, so, we told them, "Um, this is the first time I hear this, I did not know anything. How can you do this to me?" They said, "You did not know anything because you do not care about your child, but this happened, we sent you hundreds of letters during all this time, and it has been two years, and you ignored the letters." So, my husband comes home and asks me, "Did you know anything about those letters?" and I said, "I have never seen them, I have never read them, I have never responded to those letters, because I never had them in my hands." So Diego told us, "I signed the letters, I responded to those letters, I took them to the school." So I ignored all that, we are the parents, and we did not know anything. So they said, "If you do not take care of this, if Diego continues to miss school days, or if he takes any of his classmates with him, you either go to jail or you have to pay fifty (50) dollars every time he misses a school day."

I: Uh-huh...

P: No, so my husband was very angry, and he was harsh on him, he applied mano dura (hard hand) and that was when he started seeing a psychologist, and you helped us, and he was doing well for a while, actually he got a lot better but (pause).

I: Did they send him to court?

P: Yes, they sent him to court, they sent him to court, and then he went to Mexico, and tried to study there...

I: He went to Mexico after I saw him...

P: Yes, yes...

I: How long he was in Mexico... ?

P: Like two months...

I: Oh two months...

P: He could not study there...

I: Why?

P: Because, he did not transfer his classes, he did not have any documentation, no, and here he could not get any documents, um, he had to get that at the consulate, and transfer the classes he took. So, he, um, it was very frustrating too, he could not do anything, and he came back, he was not even two months there, he did not get used to be there...

I: Was he with your parents?

P: With my parents, yes, he was happy because they adore him, and they went to places, here and there but (pause).

I: But he could not go to school...

P: School, um, no, and everybody was at school, he was bored because he was at home all the time...

I: So he decided to come back.

P: He came back, and, um my husband went to court and appealed because he was in Mexico and so it was, they closed his case.

I: That is good...

P: They closed his case, and he came back, so after all that, one time, he was going to work, to the restaurant, and the police stopped him because he was over speeding. They found all his record again, and they put him in jail. He was arrested, but he was a minor, so they were supposed to study his case to know what happened with him. They did not study his case, so he was in jail that Friday (the day he was going to work), he was in jail all that Friday since 2:00 in the afternoon, all that Friday in the afternoon, all Saturday (pause).

I: Because it was a weekend...

P: Yes, a weekend, and all Sunday, and Monday morning. We went there to talk with them and they said he could not leave, they said he had to stay there until Monday morning to be seen by the judge but he was in a very small room, very lonely, I do not know if they arrest other people there, he was by himself in a room...

I: Here in town?

P: Yes, here in town, in this county, so Monday morning they called us at seven in the morning, the judge called and said she wanted to talk with my husband, and he said, "I am his guardian, I am Diego's guardian, I am his Father." They said, "Okay, you have to come pick him up." My husband asked them, "Do we have to pay anything do we have to go to court?" She said, "No, you have to come pick him up immediately." So, my husband went to pick him up and they said they apologized but he should not have been arrested (pause).

I: How was that?

P: Well, they did not review his case, and his case was closed.

I: And they arrested just for over speeding?

P: For over speeding, and they found his previous record that was supposed to be closed. They said that, they apologized to us, they said he should have been arrested only that Friday, and leave at night, just a few hours, instead of having him the whole weekend. So *they said they did not want Diego to sue them*, he could have sued them but my husband said, "Why are we going to get in trouble when you are the one who brought all this trouble? We are not going to do anything. We better go home." They (the court system) did not receive food for him (pause).

I: Are you saying that when he in jail he could not have anything eat?

P: Yes, they said we could not, but there was a man there, and he gave him hamburgers, for two days, he gave him hamburgers. But Diego said, "I did not want to eat because the bathroom was next to my bed, so how I am going to eat?" But he said that he man was very nice to him, he said the man even asked him if he wanted a cigarette, but Diego said, "No, I don't smoke."

I: Are you saying that other man was in the same room with Diego?

P: No, he was watching him...

I: Oh, he was watching him...

P: Yes, the man was there the whole weekend, with a woman, so I think they took turns, when the woman left, the man was there, when the man left the woman was there. Sometimes they were together, but, um, they had a person in that little office all the time. It was a little office, and that little room, it was ugly, with a bathroom, and a little bed, so we went to see him, they let us see him but, the judge let him go on Monday at 8:00 in the morning, before she went to court Diego left, to avoid any problems I imagine...

I: That is good...

P: So my husband brought him home and told him, "Look, is this what you want? Do you want this? You do not want to go to school, you do not want to work, what do you want?" Diego said, "No, I was going to work, I was late, and sped up until they stopped me."

I: So when he came back from Mexico he did not go to school he went to work.

P: He did not go back to school.

I: And how old he was at that time...you said he was a minor?

P: Seventeen years old...

I: What made him decide not to go to school and go to work instead?

P: He did not want to go to school. I found a program for him to study at home, um, a school counselor helped me. We applied, when they were going to send me everything and I was about to pay, um, I think I was going to make a down payment of $3,000 dollars, for the books, and um, we had a computer so we told him (Diego) he had to study at home. Then, he said, "No, I do not want to, do not spend money on me, I want to work, I am not going to study, I am going to get my GED, do not spend money on me."

I: What was that program about? Did you say home school?

P: Yes home school...

I: Uh-huh, and it has books so you can study by yourself?

P: Yes, he can study by himself, at home, and his tests are on the computer...

I: Is that program part of the school, or part of the school system, or it is out of the school system?

P: I believe it is something separate, but it is part of the government, the state, but it is a program for kids who want to study at home.

I: Is there any requirement to qualify or it is just for anybody?

P: Um, sometimes, when, because he was a "niño problema" (problem kid) so they said, "You can study at home." Yes, because, he did not want to, he was going to do, um, so the school said, "We do not want him here anymore because..."

I: But was he expelled from the school or suspended?

P: No, he was not expelled, he was suspended but we did not know it...

I: Did he have in school suspension (ISS) or out of school suspension (OSS)?

P: I think he had out of school suspension (OSS) but he did not stay at home, we were not aware of that, he went out with his friends, but yes, he received out of school suspensions (OSS), and sometimes he had in school suspension (ISS) he was at the principal's office for hours.

I: Have you ever been to the school? Have you ever talked with anybody at the school? If so, who did you talk with? Did you talk with a principal, a teacher?

P: The principal, I mean, the principal was a man, and I talked with the principal assistant, when I saw him (Diego) in school suspension. I told my husband, "Let us go to the school and see how Diego is doing." So, we went to the school. They said, no, um, this was like, six months after he started high school. So, she said, "He is not doing too bad, um, he is not doing well with his classes, and we want him to pay more attention, but he is very good in sports, he has a lot of friends, he is a very popular kid, everybody likes him a lot here, the teachers speak highly of him." I said, "Well, just because you like him a lot, or because you get along with him, does not mean he is doing well in school, that he will make him pass grades, or he is a good kid." He probably thought that getting along with his teachers would make him pass grades (pause).

I: Uh-huh, so you talked with this person, and how was that, do you speak English?,

P: No...

I: So, do they have an interpreter, do they speak Spanish, how did you communicate?

P: No, in English, everything was in English...

I: And did you understand her?

P: No, I did not understand her, my husband speaks English...

I: Oh, your husband speaks English.

P: Yes, he does speak English.

I: Okay and they do not provide an interpreter for parents who do not speak English...

P: I guess, but at that moment, we did not ask, they did not offer, and so...

I: Oh, okay.

P: So, um, when we were going to take him out of school, after all that happened, we talked with a school counselor. My husband and I went to the school to talk with them, they wanted us to say that he was going to leave the school, I mean, like "Diego is not going back to school, he is not going to attend school, anymore, he is going to start a home-school program..."

I: They wanted you to say that...

P: I think so, but I could not take him out of school, because of his age, he was about to be seventeen years old, he had to go to school, so they said, "After the break, he is going to be eighteen years old, so then you can take him out of school."

I: Uh-huh...

P: So we told them, they sent us downstairs, we went to talk with somebody else, because, I, I wanted him to stay in school, even if he was eighteen. So he said, "Look, he can stay in this school, that is not a problem, but he has to promise he is going to cooperate, and when he is eighteen years old, it does not make any sense for him to stay here." So they said, "Home school is better for him, you have to supervise him, you have to watch him, you have to demand of him, because he is going to be home studying, working on school projects, and you will know what he is doing, he is not going anywhere. We have no problem if he wants to stay in school, but he has to come to study, not to play, or miss school days."

I: Uh-huh.

P: So they said, "Well, if you want him to stay here that is fine, but home school would be his best option, we are not running him off, but we cannot handle him, and you cannot handle him, so we have to make some drastic decisions, he has court, he has to go to court." So we took him to court, he had several court days. We went to court one day, the judge grumbled to me, that was horrible, she grumbled to him, and said, she said to him, "Look, your mother is Mexican, she is not a US citizen, she is *illegal*, your father is *illegal*, you should not be in this country, and you do not even want to go to school. You know what I can do? I can send you back to your country, with your mom and dad." So Diego told her, "They have a job here," and she said, "What do they have?" He said, "They have their own business." So the judge said, "I can take their business away from them and send you back to your country with nothing in your hands, you want that?"

I: Did the judge say that?

P: Yes, I think she said it to make Diego understand his situation. Like saying, it is your fault if your parents are sent back to your country, with nothing, we will take everything from them. She said, "Do you want that for your mom and dad?" He said, "No, of course not." So she said, "I want you to be aware of your situation, if you go to school you have to study, if you do not go to school you have to study at home, and stop instigating other kids to miss school." So he said, "I do not force them to go with me, I have never forced anybody, they came with me whenever they wanted, sometimes I did not even want to go and they asked me to take them to places." So she said, "Well, nobody forced you either, you have been a bad boy because you wanted to be a bad boy, and again, if you want that for your parents, we will do that." She grumbled to him and she grumbled to me. We left court and I told him, "You see what happened?" I grumbled to him, so we left court, that day I believe I just paid 110 dollars, we left court, and they gave him another court day.

I: The reason he was in court was truancy, right? Did he have any other problems?

P: No...

I: He did not have any problems with drugs, or alcohol, or misbehavior.

P: No, never, not even fighting with somebody...

I: So he did not have any behavioral problems. The only problem was missing truancy.

P: No, he did not go to class, so when someone misses class it is because they are sick, or their parents want them to interpret for them somewhere, or because they have to work, but no (pause).

I: It was not the case...

P: No, actually, he did not even work, and when he had to work, he said, "No, I cannot help you because I have to go to school," and we thought he went to school, we said, "Oh, yes, if you have to study, go to school." But, in fact, he did not, he did not have any behavioral problems, he was not rude, he did not use drugs, or alcohol...

I: And when you told me you gave him a car, a cell phone, some freedom, what do you think about that, I mean, now looking back to that time?

P: Well, that is what we tell him, I tell him, "Look Diego, we made a mistake giving you all that, because for that reason you started doing bad things, you took the wrong way." He said, "No, it was fine, I just wanted to go out with my buddies, we wanted to be different, so we did different things, but it was not bad. I, I never used that money for drugs or alcohol; I just used that money for gas and food. As for the cell phone, you called me to find me, I told you 'I am playing football or soccer or I am here.' As for the car, I just used it to go to school." Actually, he did not even go to school. That is what I tell my husband, we made a mistake, because, we gave him all, like, like *we bought him with money to make him feel good*, but we thought he was doing well in school. We rewarded him, and because we could not take him to and from school, we told him, "Here you have your car, your cell phone, your money." Now, that I look back at things, my husband says, "We did not do anything wrong," but I think that think all that was very wrong. I tell him (husband), that was very wrong because, when kids want something, we as parents should wait for them to be older, or when you see a result of something, you may reward them, but we rewarded him before seeing anything...

I: Did he ask for those things? Or you gave them to him without asking?

P: No, he asked, he said, "Look I do not want to take the bus anymore, um, there is a guy, I was about to fight with him, he is very problematic." The guy was a "bolillo," a white American guy (bolillo is white Mexican bread. It is, also, a slang Mexican term to refer to white Americans). So he said, "I do not want to go to school, um, and plus the bus runs too early, an hour before I go to class, and um, I am riding for an hour all around the city, so." So, we had an extra car here, we already had it, it is not that we bought the car for him, we had it here, and we did not use it. So he said, "If you give me that car to go to school, I can go to work earlier, and will help you." We said, Okay, and gave him the car, and um, my cell phone did not work at that time, so we bought a new cell phone, and then that old cell phone worked. He said, "That cell phone, can I have that cell phone, the one mom had?" We said, "Okay take it..."

I: Okay, it was like a series of things, like a process of...

P: (Interrupting). Yes, like a process of, it was not, as if we said, "Oh, we have money, take this car, this cell phone."

I: Uh-huh, he was asking, you had it, so you were negotiating, right?

P: Exactly, so, um, he helped us with the little boy, when we were working hard, and the store was full of people. We were very busy, he played with his little brother, he would take him to an area with no cars and he played with him. The van had a TV, so they stayed in the truck, so in some ways he helped us, we never wanted to get a baby sitter. I always, actually, I used to babysit children, but I said, "Nobody will babysit children like me." We have seen so many bad things that we never had a babysitter. So, he watched his little brother, after class he came to work and that was his way to help us. Sometimes we said, "Hey, listen, those customers need sodas, go take some sodas to them," and he did that, he served sodas to the customers, that was the way he helped us, but he never cooked, he never had to work hard.

I: Uh-huh, and do you remember any situation in the school, any other contact you made with the school, did they call you or send you the 'report card', with his grades, how was the communication with the school?

P: No, I just went, actually, in high school, I have only been there like four times. Two times to get him registered, and the other two times to talk when, when they told us about the problems he had. We went to talk with a bunch of people, the last time we went to talk with several people to tell them we were going to take him out of school to start home school. I have been to the school in four different occasions, the other times were for sports, I went to watch him play, we were at the school, he played in his school team, but those were the only times I have contacted those people, and it was in English, they never got an interpreter for me.

I: And you never asked them to have an interpreter, they never offered you to have an interpreter, or... ?

P: (Interrupting). I never asked them, they never offered me, I had, I had a brief contact with the school, as a parent, I feel like it was not, I feel like I did not have any connection with the school.

I: And what do you think about that? I mean, was that because you did not try to connect with them, they did not call you, or both things, what was the reason?

P: Um, I did not, I felt like I did not need to go to the school because, if he was doing well, I would not do anything. I would ignore it, but when he had problems, Diego took care of everything and I did not know anything. He signed the letters, turned them in, wrote letters, I was completely unaware, so his father, and he did, when my husband was angry or something, he would say, "No, I am going to go to the school, I am going to ask them how you are doing." Diego said, "I am doing well, look, here are my grades" (pause).

I: And how were his grades?

P: His grades were, um, the first year, all his first year and the first half of the second year he was doing fine. Then, the next years, he never showed us anything. I asked him, "Where is your report card?" He said, "Um, I got it but I already turned it back in." So we never saw it, we did not know how he was doing, and when I went to the school to get him registered, they just said, "Oh, you have to sign here, he is going to take these and these classes, he is going to repeat these." So, but, I was never completely informed about school, and plus I did not like going to school because of the language, they did not have an interpreter for me, they did not offer an interpreter for me, I had to understand what they said no matter what...

I: You did not feel comfortable saying, "I need an interpreter" or "I would feel more comfortable with an interpreter"?

P: No, because, like I said, I have been there twice to get him registered, two to talk with them. My husband and I went to the school a couple of times to pick him up to take him to the doctor. I just went to the school and said, "I need to talk with Diego." They said, "Diego's mom is here." We signed, I signed and we left, he went back to school or I would say, "He is gone for today." That was it. I have never been to the school to get information or anything like that, neither my husband. When my friends started telling me about their problems with their kids, I said, "Oh, no, Diego is doing fine, he has no problems at school," maybe they did know that he had problems and did not say anything to me. I said, "Diego goes to school, he is not doing perfect, but he is doing fine at school." I have never investigated anything about him, and that was a huge mistake, I am not going to make the same mistake with my younger son, I do not understand the language but I tell him, "Tell your teacher this or tell your teacher I want to know how you are doing."

I: You can always request an interpreter; you have a right to have an interpreter.

P: I do not think they have an interpreter but I guess then may find one over the phone...

I: I think you have the right to have an interpreter at a hospital, at school; it is your right...

P: Yes, in my younger son's school there are a few Hispanics, I think they only have ten Hispanic students so (pause).

I: It does not matter, even if they have *one* Hispanic student, they should provide an interpreter for those parents who do not speak the language.

P: Yes, but I am not going to make the same mistake, I check on him al the time, I check on, him, I check on him. He is an outstanding student, he is doing very well in school, he is praised by teachers, and like I said, I am not going to wait like I did with Diego because that was a bad experience, and I was very frustrated because I think that if I had done more things maybe he would have finished high school. Although, he says that is not true, he says that school is *not* for him, and he was not going to finish high school anyway.

I: Uh-huh.

P: He does not like school, he said he never liked school, he had friends, they did terrible in school, they had really bad grades; they even said they went to school to warm the chair up (calentar el banco) but they all got their GED. They did horribly, terribly, but they all got their GED, and he did not (pause).

I: Well, he may decide to get it sometime in the future, right?

P: Yes, exactly, I am very excited about him getting the GED, and I would like him to study something. His father went to investigate here at the *Technologic school* and they said he can study there, with a GED, he can get a technical degree in electro mechanic, engineering...

I: That is good...would he like to do that?

P: No, he does not want to do that, we told him we could pay for him to go to college, but he does not want to do that...

I: It sounds like he wants to work now... .

P: Um, sometimes he says he is tired and bored of working...

I: Well, he can change his mind, he is young...Let me ask you this, what are your expectations for him as a mother?

P: Well, like any dreamer mom, I would like him to get married, to have his family and at least to have a technical degree, a career, short but something to be able to defend himself, here. Because, he does not have a social security, if we do not have any documents to be in this country so we are a Don Nadie

(Mr. Nobody), right? And without a degree, it is even worse. What helps him a lot is that he speaks English, and he is a very charismatic child, he has, he has a lot of, um, he is very good communicating with people, he has good manners (don de gentes)...

I: He is very nice...

P: Yes, and people treat him well anywhere. Americans, Hispanics, but I would like for him that, um to grow as a person, so that he could get at least a short career. He is going to be a dad, he has a girlfriend, the girl is pregnant, they became independent, they live together, they pay their bills, I tell him, "Well, that is perfect, but I would like for you to marry her."

I: Tell me about that, I do not know that, I am from Argentina; is it important for you to get married instead of living together? How is it in your culture?

P: In our culture, um, if you get married, you comply with your partner; you can be with that person all the time, but with God's laws, and with civil laws. Yes, you protect your children, if you get divorced, your children will be unprotected, and without a father, without papers. You have your father and mother's last names. In a marriage, otherwise, we are natural children, you are only your mom's child, you have your mom's last name. So, yes, in our culture getting married is something very good, so you have your documents as a couple, and your children are protected. If you are not there, if the father is not there, children have rights to get things from their father, or a good last name, and to be a child within the marriage, but um, he agrees with the American liberalism ideas...

I: Say more about that...

P: Well, he is like Americans, he says, "No, I do not need a piece of paper, I do not want to get married." And his girlfriend says that, too. She says, "Now, we love each other, and if we do not love each other anymore we can part ways" (pause).

I: Do you believe Americans do that... ?

P: No, I do not believe that...

I: So why did you say that he agrees with the American liberalism ideas...some Americans get married...they like getting married...

P: Really?

I: I guess.

P: But the kids at school, his classmates, they are seventeen, eighteen years old, they have their girlfriends, they make them pregnant and leave. They start dating other people, the girls start dating other men, they do not live together, the babies live with their grandparents. He did not do that when he was in school, but he is doing it now that he left school...

I: Uh-huh, I thought you were talking about living together. Something I noticed about Hispanics is that they live together but consider that as "being married," they say "my wife" or "my husband," I respect that...

P: Yes, yes, in fact, they do that, most of the Hispanics like 'cohabitation' (union libre)...

I: They cohabitate sometimes for 20, 30 years...

P: Yes, but some people cohabitate and they leave and cohabitate with somebody else and...

I: It could be, it could be...

P: And they do not care about their kids, and then there is a lot of children with different dads and moms and so, and Americans do that, they are married and they are with other people. We, Hispanics are more conservative, the family is more traditional, my husband's family is all about getting married, my family, too.

There is all kind of people from all over the world, and there are people who only like cohabitation, but I do not agree with that...

I: You do not agree with that.

P: I do not agree with that, we told Diego, he asked his girlfriend's hand, they have been together for four years...

I: Is there anything else you want to tell me?

P: No, I do not think so.

I: Thank you very much for your time!

P: You are welcome and anything else you need we are here.

I: Thank you again.

www.ingramcontent.com/pod-product-compliance
Lightning Source LLC
Chambersburg PA
CBHW020912290526
45784CB00002BA/524